P9-CAU-618

THE
BROOKLYN
Dodgers

THE BROOKLYN Dodgers

Peter C. Bjarkman

CHARTWELL
BOOKS, INC.

Published by
CHARTWELL BOOKS INC.
A Division of **BOOK SALES, INC.**
110 Enterprise Avenue
Secaucus, New Jersey 07094

Produced by
Brompton Books Corp.
15 Sherwood Place
Greenwich, CT 06830

Copyright © 1992 Brompton Books Corp.

All rights reserved. No part of this publication may be reproduced, stored in a retrieval system or transmitted in any form by any means, electronic, mechanical, photocopying or otherwise, without first obtaining the written permission of the copyright owner.

ISBN 1-55521-761-3

Printed in Hong Kong

ACKNOWLEDGMENTS

The author and publisher would like to thank the following people who helped in the preparation of this book: Don Longabucco, the designer; Susan Bernstein, the editor; and Rita Longabucco, the picture editor.

For Ira Bring, who never let the word "Yankees" be spoken in the house!

PHOTO CREDITS

All photographs courtesy UPI/Bettmann Newsphotos except the following:
Brompton Photo Library: pages 3, 7(top left, bottom right), 66, 79.
Carl Kidwiler: pages 7(top right), 52, 54(top left), 61(bottom).
National Baseball Library, Cooperstown, NY: pages 10, 15, 16, 20, 29(top), 30(bottom), 40(top), 44(right), 48(top), 65(bottom right).
© TV Sports Mailbag, Elmsford, NY: pages 2, 6, 50, 51, 54(top right, bottom left and right), 55, 62, 63, 74, 78.

Page 1: *Round-the-horn double play kills another Brooklyn World Series threat in Game Two Ebbets Field action during the 1956 Fall Classic.*

Page 2: *No player is more intimately associated with the Brooklyn baseball club than pioneering black star Jackie Robinson.*

Page 3: *Unsung turn-of-the-century hurler Nap Rucker strikes a classic cigarette card pose.*

These pages: *Brooklyn's first 20th-century league championship outfit poses for a team portrait only weeks before the Robins' first-ever World Series appearance in 1916.*

CONTENTS

INTRODUCTION: THE MYSTERY OF "AMERICA'S TEAM"

If most old-fashioned baseball fans seem to be repelled by the corporate image of the staid New York Yankees, it appears as though almost everyone still loves the long-since-departed Dodgers from Brooklyn. As someone once phrased it, if rooting for the Yankees was somewhat like pulling for U.S. Steel, being a Dodgers fan in Brooklyn was always a passionate affair. From their earliest days, the Brooklyn Bums have held a special charm for fans.

Although the Dodgers ceased to exist as a team in 1957, and their beloved shrine, Ebbets Field, was leveled by urban development in 1960, the memory of the now silent Dodgers has gained strength across the decades, seemingly serving as a metaphor for the belief that professional baseball teams are public property. This nostalgic history is an attempt to capture some of the reasons why that long-departed Dodgers team was able to weave a special kind of magic throughout the baseball world.

If you grew up a baseball fan between the first rumblings of the Second World War at the end of the 1930s and the height of the Cold War in the mid-1950s, there was no more

Left: *Dodgers pitcher Ralph Branca grabs Giant Bobby Thomson by the throat in this photo taken shortly after Thomson's famous 1951 pennant-winning homer off of Branca.*

Opposite top left: *Gil Hodges – baseball's best first sacker of the golden 1950s – today remains the most inexplicable and unjustified oversight of Cooperstown voters.*

Opposite top right: *Reese was a man of unforgettable nicknames – Pee Wee, The Little Colonel, Captain – and of magical plays in the field and at bat.*

Opposite bottom right: *Jackie Robinson was the inspiration and spirit of the fiery "Boys of Summer" teams – a man who brought pennants to Brooklyn and respectability to the entire baseball world.*

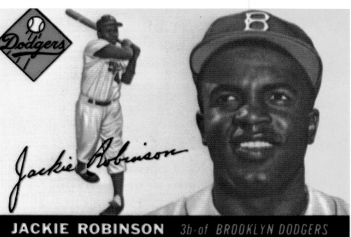

JACKIE ROBINSON   3b-of BROOKLYN DODGERS

glorious team than the Dodgers of Brooklyn. From the days of Lippy Durocher, through the reign of Branch Rickey, to the fence-busting "Boys of Summer" teams that annually battled the New York Yankees in the tension-packed Subway Series play that highlighted October baseball of the 1950s, the Dodgers cast their spell across the East Coast and all of America. They were the closest thing to what might be called "America's Team" in the national pastime.

Even in baseball's greatest season — a half century ago in 1941 — the baseball world was as much focused on tiny Ebbets Field as it was on the slugging of the Yankee Clipper in the Bronx or the Splendid Splinter in Beantown. As we celebrate the 50th anniversary of baseball's most joyous summer, we lionize the streak of DiMaggio and the .400 hitting assault of Williams. But we tend to forget that it was really the Dodgers that captured the fancy of baseball's several million fans that summer. Baseball historian Robert Creamer has reminded us that against the backdrop of DiMaggio and Williams's celebrated mano-a-mano battle, it was Brooklyn's darlings under Durocher who were the true Cinderella team.

And as postwar America returned to normal and then moved into the greatest boom era of the nation's history, the Brooklyn Dodgers rose alongside the Yankees in baseball's greatest dual-dynasty reign. The Yankees of that era, of course, still stand as baseball's juggernaut. Five times in a row Stengel's men were world champions. And then after a brief spell, Stengel and his boys launched another five-year streak. And through the first half of this unprecedented Yankees decade it was almost always the Dodgers who were the annual challenger and the annual victim. In baseball's true golden decade the game was focused on the city of New York. The great teams were there,

and the great stars — Mantle, Snider, Ford, Robinson, Berra, Reese, and dozens more wore Yankee pinstripes or Brooklyn blue. Since the Dodgers were always bridesmaids to the Yankees, they inevitably emerged from the decade as baseball's most tragic and consistent losers.

But memory fails in its persistent efforts to reconstitute history, and the "Boys of Summer" Dodgers were anything but wretched losers. Not only were they the second best team in New York between 1947 and 1957 but perhaps the second best team in the entire annals of baseball. The record is indisputable on the Dodgers' total domination of the senior circuit during the "Boys of Summer" era: six league pennants in less than a dozen summers; four more campaigns in the runner-up slot, with the margin of defeat

only once reaching more than three games; a single slip to third place. And this team not only won. It flaunted a cast of the most colorful baseball figures the game has known. Even the front office and the bench sparkled with the innovations and antics of such stormy pioneers as Hurricane Larry MacPhail, champion of night-time baseball; the "Old Mahatma" Branch Rickey, the shrewdest judge of diamond talent the game has ever seen; and incorrigible Leo Durocher, the rebel manager of the Dodgers who drove both nearly to distraction.

But still, it was on the ball field that the Dodgers captured the public imagination. And in that memorable period from World War II until Sputnik, almost every position in the Dodgers lineup was staffed by a colorful and inspired hero. Campanella stood as an immovable rock behind home plate. Hodges was the game's unparalleled first sacker and the most overlooked superstar of the era. Jackie Robinson flashed across baseball from one outfield and three infield positions. Billy Cox was a magician at the hot corner, while Pee Wee Reese was the true idol of hometown Brooklyn fans. The greatest and most controversial figure of all was the

slugging Duke of Flatbush who roamed the center field pastures with incomparable grace and unrivaled skill.

There were lesser figures, as well, who made the Dodgers exciting and flamboyant. Carl Furillo was without peer at his position in right field and enjoyed a special relationship with the Brooklyn fans. He was a nuts-and-bolts laborer – a true hardhat ball player. Carl Erskine (Oisk) had a nickname that inspired familial loyalties. Towering Don Newcombe – the first dominant black pitcher – was an imposing yet controversial hurler, as much a pioneer as Jackie or Campy and yet a moody ball player who might fold under pressure and lose the clutch games. Preacher Roe was a master moundsman who spun webs of magic over league hitters for a few brief seasons yet maintained the guise of a simple country boy. If the Yankees were all business, the Dodgers were color and thrills.

Before the glory years of the 1940s and 1950s, Brooklyn teams had a far different image – less ennobling if nonetheless colorful. The first three decades of the 20th century brought a seemingly endless string of pennant failures and an indelible image captured by the club's previous informal

Left: *Hodges and Robinson kick up Ebbets Field dust in a sliding exhibition for the willing cameraman.*

Above: *Leo Durocher and his charges seem anything but somber after the 1946 playoff defeat by the Cards.*

nickname — "Dem Bums." But they were lovable bums, indeed. And a reputation for ineptitude soon became a license for the relentless folly of the Daffiness Dodgers of the 1930s era. This was the ball club that boasted Babe Herman and Hack Wilson — free-swinging sluggers with iron bats, lead gloves, and concrete baseball minds. It was the team that once actually saw three men hugging third simultaneously. And it was the team that never failed eventually to break the hearts of its faithful.

It may seem strange more than three decades after the final ball game played in Brooklyn that a dead baseball franchise could still capture the imagination of the nation's baseball millions, many of whom never saw the team in the flesh. Other moribund franchises are buried and forgotten. Boston's Braves, Philadelphia's Athletics, the hapless St. Louis Browns, even the unpredictable New York Giants are all the mere dust of old baseball history books. Yet the Dodgers somehow live anew each season, demonstrating that Abner Doubleday's sport is more a game of embellished myth than of bare-bones history.

There may be several explanations for the phenomenon of the Brooklyn Dodgers. In part it may be simply the baseball nostalgia that marks the early years of the 1990s. Most fans over 40 long for an earlier age when the game was heard on radio, when the sky was not covered by plastic domes and the grass was still real, and when the heroes were in touch with their adoring fans. There is also the fact that the Brooklyn Dodgers mirrored a sprawling city of millions who for nearly five decades took their identity from a proud local ball club — and in some perverse sense still do. Never before has any sports franchise been so in tune with the community that supported it.

Then there is the undeniable fact that baseball fans love losers. Not hopeless also-rans like the St. Louis Browns, or the worst of Connie Mack's Philadelphia teams, or the rash of expansion bums foisted on Kansas City in the 1950s — Montreal and San Diego in the 1960s, or Seattle and Toronto in the late 1970s. But those near-winners, last-second losers who learn life's painful lessons of eleventh-hour defeat wrenched time and again from the jaws of expected victory. Teams like the Red Sox of Boston, the Cubs of Chicago, or the Tigers of Detroit — proud challengers that always find a way to raise expectations and then dash them ruthlessly in the final inning of the season's final weekend.

When it comes to such tragic losers, the team that represented Brooklyn in the days of Rickey, Robinson, Reese, and Snider is almost in a class by itself. This is the club that suffered the most famous last-second pennant defeat in history — Bobby Thomson's homer, which propelled the hated crosstown Giants to unlikely triumph in 1951. It was the team that had lost in almost identical fashion the season before — snake-bit by Dick Sisler and the miracle Whiz Kid Phillies. It is the team that ran away from the National League pack year after year and then inexplicably crumbled in October before the Yankees.

But perhaps the best reason for the Dodgers' endless popularity remains the colorful ballplayers who wore Brooklyn colors. First there were men like Zack Wheat, Casey Stengel, Wilbert Robinson, and Babe Herman — diamond figures both zany and charismatic. Soon followed the game's most storied pioneer, Jackie Robinson. And in Robinson's wake came Campanella, who battled fiercely yet so quietly. And also the stoic Reese, who showed such peerless leadership. And the fence-busting hitters like Snider, Hodges, and Furillo, who together filled Ebbets Field with long balls and graceful defensive plays. This book is their story. And in it, one of baseball's unforgettable teams can live once more in the fan's imagination — the one place where they will never die.

1. TROLLEY DODGERS, BRIDEGROOMS, AND A GENIUS NAMED EBBETS

Team nicknames were something that Dodgers outfits of an earlier age in Brooklyn wore with no more regularity than championship rings. Throughout the club's first four decades a host of colorful monikers were affixed and discarded in rapid succession by the often slapstick Brooklyn nine. They began business as the "Trolley Dodgers" — it was one of the derisive gibes that sedate Manhattan islanders regularly tossed at those rival settlers across the East River who saved life and limb by dodging the menacing horse-drawn trolleys that crisscrossed Brooklyn thoroughfares. They were known for a short time in the early 1890s as the "Bridegrooms," or "Grooms" for short, supposedly because a stock of Brooklyn players all marched to the altar during the same summer season of 1889. But soon they were known alternately as "Ward's Wonders," for their moderately successful manager John Montgomery Ward during early National League days, or as "Foutz's Fillies," after the less successful Dave Foutz, who followed Hall-of-Famer Ward to the Brooklyn bench in the mid-1890s.

An unexpected infusion of former Baltimore Orioles stars in 1899 and 1900 soon brought a brief cluster of championship pennants and a new appellation as well – this time in honor of skillful manager Ned Hanlon. A popular touring vaudeville act known as Hanlon's Superbas provided an irresistible moniker for the Brooklyn National League club during Ned Hanlon's seven-year reign between 1899 and 1905. And since the tradition of the day of extracting team nicknames from popular field managers was so rampant within the baseball press, for most of the 18-year reign (1915-1931) of popular Wilbert Robinson ("Uncle Robbie" to players, fans, and writers alike), the Brooklyns were fittingly referred to by baseball reporters also as "Robins," especially in the pages of the Brooklyn *Eagle*. The name "Dodgers" was in vogue from time to time as well, but its full currency as the official team identity was not established until shortly after Robinson's firing in 1931.

But among the hoards of Brooklyn faithful, the true name for their beloved charges was never really plain "Dodgers" anyway, even after Uncle Robbie's departure from the Brooklyn baseball scene. That honor belongs to a popular label that had stuck to the club in press column and grandstand during the earliest Depression years. For most Flatbush rooters of the final three Brooklyn decades, the Dodgers were accepted simply as "Dem Lovable Bums" – an image so endeared by Brooklyn fans that even the sober Walter O'Malley was loathe to lobby against it.

"Bums" – as several Dodgers historians have hastened to recount – was an improbable nickname. Contemporary newspaper accounts have it that a certain Brooklyn diehard of the Depression era took special pleasure in loudly bemoaning the inept play of the local team from his safe refuge in the box seats behind home plate. This leather-lunged fan held sway for several seasons with one particular favorite epithet – "Ya bum, ya" – usually directed gener-

Opposite: *A proud Mrs. Ed McKeever, wife of the Brooklyn ball club's vice-president, hoists a new flag for the first game at Ebbets Field on April 9, 1913.*

Above: *Manager Wilbert Robinson (in topcoat) surveys his "Daffiness Boys" during spring practice sessions.*

Left: *Charlie Ebbets poses with his new bride (c) and the wife of pitcher Dutch Ruether (r) in this May 1922 domestic scene.*

Overleaf: *Ebbets Field, Brooklyn's incomparable baseball shrine, captured in all its stately charm during the 1949 season. Like all urban parks of its era, Ebbets Field was perfectly molded to the contours of a city block.*

ously at each member of the Brooklyn team. Local baseball writer Sid Mercer was especially taken with this boisterous rooter. He dubbed him "the spirit of Brooklyn" and picked up the popular local expletive in his daily reportage of Dodgers games. "Bums Win" or "Bums Lose" was soon a familiar headline on the sports pages of the Brooklyn *Eagle*.

But it remained for New York sports cartoonist Willard Mullin to create the image of the pudgy hobo — with his characteristic cigar stub, bearded chin, and tattered jacket — that was to become the unofficial Dodger logo by the onset of World War II. Owner Walter O'Malley, always able to recognize a good marketing gimmick, eventually employed Mullin to draw his shabby mascot for the covers of team yearbooks and press guides. Like no other professional baseball club, the Dodgers of Brooklyn were a true community institution and it was the fans of Brooklyn themselves who honored the team with an identity of their own popular choosing.

While NL baseball was fittingly born in the year of the nation's centennial, it was not until 1883 that the embryonic Dodgers first emerged. This occurred when real estate executive and attorney Charles H. Byrne — purportedly at the urging of New York *Herald* editor George Taylor — decided to invest in the promising new sport that was rapidly becoming the craze of a booming industrial nation. Byrne, with financial backing from known gamblers Joe Doyle and Gus Abell, entered his new team in the short-lived Interstate League, having hurriedly constructed a makeshift ballpark on a site where George Washington had once fought a key Revolutionary War battle. Entrenched in their new ballpark (often credited as the nation's first enclosed ball yard), Brooklyn's inaugural "Dodgers" walked away with a pennant in that first and only season of Interstate League play.

Buoyed by such immediate success, Byrne transferred his team to the more established American Association for the following season, an overly ambitious move that saw his club dashed to a ninth-place finish in the older 12-team circuit. While a lasting tradition of winning baseball was certainly not born in these earliest American Association years, the nickname "Dodgers" did come to common currency. The disparaging appellation "Trolley Dodgers" quickly stuck to the common citizens of Brooklyn borough,

as well as to the professional ball club which now represented borough pride. It continued for some time to share equal currency with more standard baseball nicknames such as Bridegrooms, Brooklyns, Brooklyners, or simply Brooks.

The 1890s also witnessed the rise of the borough's first remarkable baseball personality. Charles Hercules Ebbets, an intelligent, affable, and ambitious young businessman who came into the employment of Charles Byrne and his partners in 1894, would soon leave his indelible mark on the fortunes and vicissitudes of Brooklyn baseball. But Ebbets's rise to power with the Dodgers was often slow and painstaking.

One of the more memorable events of his early tenure with the Brooklyn franchise was a business transaction now somewhat hard to fathom in the frame of modern-day baseball management. Ebbets had been a loyal employee with the Brooklyn club for six years by the time the Bridegrooms joined the National League. He sold scorecards and tickets, cleaned the grandstands and the club offices, and

Left: *Charlie Ebbets (r) enjoys a playful moment of sideline conversation with baseball commissioner Kenesaw Mountain Landis. It was the crafty Ebbets who brought Ned Hanlon and his stable of high-flying Baltimore Orioles to New York and thus first put Brooklyn baseball on the National League map.*

Opposite top left: *Ned Hanlon put together one of the most famous 19th-century teams as manager of the Baltimore Orioles between 1892 and 1898. As leader of the champion Orioles he pioneered such innovations as the hit-and-run play, fielders covering for each other on defense, and full-time use of a club groundskeeper. Arriving in Brooklyn in 1899, the cunning field general quickly brought two National League pennants for the Superbas as well.*

Opposite top right: *Ned Hanlon's successes in Brooklyn can largely be attributed to a fellow refugee from Baltimore, Wee Willie Keeler, who hit .379 and .362 in his first two Brooklyn years. A native Brooklynite, Keeler possessed a formula for success which became the game's surest axiom: "Keep your eye on the ball and hit 'em where they ain't!"*

Opposite bottom: *James "Deacon" McGuire appeared in more big league seasons (26) than any catcher in baseball history, two of those coming with league champion Brooklyn clubs in 1899 and 1900.*

kept most of the financial ledgers as well. He even took over as field manager for the club for part of the 1898 season, when the tenth-place Bridegrooms reached rock bottom in their tailspin of the late 1890s.

While making himself indispensable in the front office, Ebbets also shrewdly purchased whatever available club stock his limited resources would allow. By 1897, though he owned only 10 percent of the club, Charles Ebbets was elected team president, being acknowledged by fellow owner Byrne and his various shady associates as the only knowledgeable baseball man in the organization. In the following season, his baseball acumen and business guile combined to pull off a blockbuster deal designed to transform Brooklyn baseball fortunes. Although the high-flying Baltimore Orioles were an unrivaled league champion (pennant winners in 1894-96), owner Harry Von der Horst, a Baltimore brewer with little real baseball interest, had enjoyed sparse success with his own club at the ticket gate. The crafty Ebbets, aware of Von der Horst's flagging interest, conspired to transfer majority ownership of the financially successful Brooklyn team to Von der Horst. League rules did not prevent multiple team ownership in those days. To the delight of Brooklyn rooters (and the immense satisfaction of the devious Ebbets), Von der Horst was then persuaded to enhance his new investment by shipping a cartload of his best Baltimore players to Brooklyn, along with crack manager Ned Hanlon. Paced by ex-Orioles Wee Willie Keeler, Hughie Jennings, Joe Kelley, Joe "Iron Man" McGinnity, and Jimmy Sheckard, the transformed Hanlon-lead Brooklyn team predictably swept to easy pennants in both 1899 and 1900.

Hanlon's Baltimore-flavored Brooklyn team was like a momentary supernova, launched at the end of the National League's own brief monopoly on professional baseball. In 1901 a rival American League was put in place and the new

eight-club circuit immediately set to work raiding rosters of the established National League rivals, just as the short-lived Players' League had done a decade earlier. No club was more damaged in the crossfire than Brooklyn (which had similarly suffered during the Players' League Wars), with outfield standouts Keeler and Kelley and pitching stars McGinnity and Wild Bill Donovan immediately jumping to the new high-paying league. Ned Hanlon's teams soon tumbled to fifth (1903), sixth (1904), and eighth (1905), losing 105 games in his final season of 1905 and finishing 56½ games behind the pace-setting World Champion Giants. That the rival New Yorkers had emerged as baseball's newest powerhouse under John J. McGraw, while Ned Hanlon's Superbas (formerly the Bridegrooms) stumbled to the league's basement, was particularly galling to the Brooklyn faithful.

Yet Charles Ebbets himself had little reason to grieve. Ebbets had finally bought out Von der Horst with borrowed funds in 1904 and now was virtually sole owner of the ball club. He had immediately re-elected himself club president, raised his own salary from $4000 to $10,000 and cut the

annual paycheck of his field manager from $11,500 to $7500. By the conclusion of the disastrous 1905 campaign, the disgruntled Hanlon had already departed and Wild Bill Donovan's brother, Patsy Donovan, was quickly appointed the new Brooklyn skipper for the 1906 league season.

Brooklyn's roller-coaster baseball fortunes continued to dip noticeably during the post-Hanlon years — two fifth-place finishes and a seventh-place season under Donovan; a single sixth-place campaign with Harry Lumley at the helm in 1909; and two sixth-place years and two seventh-place finishes under ex-shortstop Bill Dahlen between 1910 and 1913. A National League MVP season by first baseman Jack Daubert, who hit at a .350 clip in 1913, provided a rare lift to the sagging Brooklyn fortunes. Yet Ebbets was well occupied at this time, about to hatch his grandest scheme yet. Having moved his club by 1898 into a fresh new 12,000-seat wooden stadium, renamed Washington Park and located in south Brooklyn (they had played at Eastern Park since abandoning the original Washington Park in 1891), Ebbets longed for a still larger facility with more seats and better control over paying customers. As the natural rivalry with

McGraw's crosstown Giants heated up, regularly drawing huge crowds after the turn of the century, Ebbets was acutely aware of the financial opportunity represented by a new stadium, especially one that would prevent further freeloading by the Washington Park fans. Disgruntled with the team's diminished talents, they preferred vantage points atop the surrounding tenements to paid admissions (at a mere 50 cents a ticket) in the increasingly empty ballpark bleachers.

Again borrowing heavily in order to purchase a parcel of land near the outskirts of Flatbush — smack within the murky shantytown area known to locals as "Pigtown" — Ebbets constructed his colossus of a ballpark in time for the opening of the 1913 season. The cost was steep: $750,000 for an impressive edifice, perhaps the finest in the major leagues. It was solid brick construction with great arched ornamental windows and a basilica-like rotunda entrance. Seating was available for 18,000, with additional space for 3000 standees. On April 9, 1913, Ebbets Field opened its doors to a rain-diminished crowd of 12,000, which wit-

nessed an inaugural loss of 1-0 to the Philadelphia Phillies. The unsung hero of this first Ebbets Field game was Brooklyn's Casey Stengel. The young outfielder provided the Flatbush faithful with one genuine thrill for the otherwise dreary afternoon — a spectacular first inning left field catch that nearly saved the day for hard-luck Brooklyn southpaw Nap Rucker.

Even from its maiden season of 1913, cramped and creaky Ebbets Field seemed destined to provide a setting for eccentric baseball characters, inept and often exasperating home-team play, and continuous front-office wrangling (usually accompanied by near insolvency in the team's coffers). While other New York franchises — the heroic Yankees of the Bronx and the hated Giants of Manhattan — offered troops of baseball heroes, storybook pennant campaigns, and countless memorable diamond achievements, the Bums of Flatbush spawned outlandish ragtag buffoons and insufferably long dry spells of second-division baseball fortunes. But in the process they sowed the seeds for one of baseball's enduring legends.

Opposite left: *Hall-of-Famer Joe Kelley was a lifetime .317 hitter who also starred for the four-time champion Baltimore Orioles of the 1890s and then accompanied manager Edward Hanlon north to Brooklyn in 1899. The hard-hitting outfielder was converted to a first baseman during his final Brooklyn campaign of 1901 and hit above .300 for all three seasons he labored in Flatbush.*

Opposite right: *Hurler "Iron Man" Joe McGinnity was awarded to the upstart Brooklyn franchise when Baltimore was dropped from the league in 1900. It was that very season when the side-arming hurler earned his now famous sobriquet, capturing 29 games for Hanlon's Brooklyn club and once posting five separate victories in but six days.*

Right: *Manager Wilbert Robinson (l) confers with captain Jake Daubert on the Ebbets Field dugout steps before a contest with the rival Giants in April 1917. Daubert was a lifetime .300 hitter and two-time NL batting champion with Brooklyn.*

2. THE DAFFINESS BOYS

Brooklyn ball players are often remembered more for the charming and often apocryphal tales that enliven their diamond exploits than for the statistics or feats they have etched into baseball's record books. As baseball historian Donald Honig once noted, baseball history will always choose the good story over plain statistics. And the essence of Brooklyn baseball history between the First and Second World Wars lies not so much in the record book but rather in the pages of pure folklore.

Unforgettable figures like Babe Herman and Casey Stengel provide the necessary test cases. That Babe Herman was one of the sport's greatest pure hitters during baseball's big

Left: *Manager Wilbert Robinson and ace hurler Dazzy Vance discuss pitching strategy at the outset of the 1926 season. Vance was just coming off two league-leading 20-win campaigns and was in the midst of his run of seven back-to-back seasons as senior circuit strikeout king. Robinson's Brooklyn club itself, however, was part way along the journey through five straight sixth-place campaigns.*

Opposite: *"Uncle Robbie" proudly raises a National League pennant flag at Ebbets Field during the 1921 Opening Day ceremonies. Assisting in the official moment is opposing manager Wild Bill Donovan of the Philadelphia Phillies, himself once a turn-of-the-century Brooklyn moundsman. Robbie's team was fresh off a 1920 World Series appearance against the Cleveland Indians.*

stick era of the 1920s and 1930s is almost totally forgotten. That Herman was at times a bumbling fielder and scatter-brained base runner is, by contrast, a commonplace of baseball lore, even when the facts (for example, that Herman became a fine fielder before his playing days had run their course) have to be stretched to fit the reality. Such glorious moments in the career of Charles Dillon Stengel as a World Series inside-the-park homer for the Giants in 1923 or a thrilling first-inning catch in the inaugural contest at Ebbets Field in 1913 have slipped completely through the cracks of history. But everyone has heard the one about Casey doffing his cap in Ebbets Field and letting loose the captive bird ensconced there.

Of course some exciting baseball was played in Ebbets Field in the summers immediately preceding and following the First World War. Much of it was played by the Brooklyn team whose checkered uniforms were perhaps the ugliest flannels ever to grace a big league diamond. First came a rare pennant in the campaign of 1916, a season that saw Zack Wheat reach the height of his vaunted slugging career (with league-leading figures for slugging average and total bases) and the Brooklyn team of third-year skipper Wilbert Robinson become the city's first ball club of the 20th century to win in excess of 90 games.

If building Ebbets Field would remain the foremost legacy of Charles Ebbets in his nearly 30 years at the helm of the Dodgers, his second greatest act was his selection of the jovial Wilbert Robinson to direct the team's on-field fortunes. Robinson, who had once starred for Baltimore's Orioles of the 1890s and whose century-old big-league record for seven hits in seven at bats during a single game still stands, assumed command as the new Brooklyn manager at the outset of the second season of play in Ebbets Field. Wilbert Robinson and Charles Ebbets were almost the ideal complementary pair to guide Brooklyn baseball fortunes. The stuffy manner of the Squire of Brooklyn, as Ebbets was widely known, was time and again offset by the rotund, good-natured, 50-plus-year-old ex-catcher. Robinson's well-established baseball image was, in fact, that of the consummate peacemaker, a role he had played well while teammate to the irascible John "Muggsy" McGraw in Baltimore and then again as McGraw's trusty coach and advisor with the NL Giants. Only an irreparable split between Robinson and McGraw brought on by bitter quarreling during the 1913 World Series gave Ebbets the opportunity to seize the talented and immensely popular Robinson for his own, and thus to inflict a small wound upon the hated McGraw and his Giants in the process. Robinson, in turn, managed to bring the Brooklyn team two pennants in his first seven seasons under Ebbets, a much welcomed improvement for a franchise that had not enjoyed regular victory since the 1900 campaign.

Robinson's early years were promising enough. The 1916 club, buoyed by a third-place 1915 finish and the acquisition of pitchers Jack Coombs from the Athletics (for whom he had won 30 games a few seasons earlier), spitball hurler Larry Cheney from the Cubs, and left-hander Rube Marquard from the Giants, held on through the summer for a scant two and one-half game pennant margin over the Phillies, themselves paced by Grover Cleveland Alexander's spectacular 33 victories.

Robinson's 1916 team was a cut above previous Brooklyn standards, yet hardly a dynasty in the making. That was demonstrated by the ease with which Brooklyn was quickly dispatched, four games to one, by the Boston Red Sox and their ace moundsman Babe Ruth, ruining Brooklyn's first-ever World Series appearance. Yet Robinson and his charges were also something more than a flash in the pan, and the 1920 club under Uncle Robbie rebounded from three disastrous wartime years (seventh in 1917 and fifth in the following two campaigns) and raced to a comfortable seven-game final margin over runner-up New York.

This time around, the Brooklyns were confident of World Series victory against the junior circuit opposition. Their opponent was a heavy-hitting Cleveland club, led by playing-manager Tris Speaker with his robust .388 batting average and league-leading 50 doubles. Yet the 1920 Series, played under an experimental five-of-nine format instituted at the outset of World War I, again proved disheartening for Brooklyn fans, the final tally being five-games-to-two in favor of the Indians. Ace spitballer Stan Coveleski shut out Brooklyn three times; only Zack Wheat (.333) and short-

shop Ivy Olsen (.320) hit with any consistency for Uncle Robbie's men, and Burleigh Grimes provided the solitary bright spot for Brooklyn by shutting down Cleveland without a run in the second Series game.

The true drama of the 1920 World Series, however, was to unfold in the remarkable fifth game, played in Cleveland's League Park on October 10, and won handily (8-1 was the final count) by the American League Indians. This single game—one of the most unforgettable in Series history—saw two unprecedented "firsts" and one spectacular "only," which more than spiced the day's play. In inning one Elmer Smith of Cleveland connected against Brooklyn ace Burleigh Grimes for a first-ever World Series grand slam homer. Not to be outdone, Cleveland hurler Jim Bagby (31-12 that season) touched Grimes as well for a three-run shot in inning three, the first homer by a pitcher in World Series play. But both hits were overshadowed by what transpired during the following inning. With Robins hugging each base, pitcher Clarence Mitchell was allowed by Uncle Robbie to bat for himself and promptly answered his skipper's faith by lining a screamer toward center field. What happened next stunned all in attendance, as Mitchell's apparent hit was miraculously speared by Indians second baseman Bill Wambsganss. Wamby reached instant immortality by converting Mitchell's smash into the only unassisted triple play in World Series annals. It is only an amusing footnote to this memorable moment that in Mitchell's next at bat that day the Brooklyn spitballer also lined into a double play, thus becoming apparently the only man in baseball history to account for five outs with just two swings of his bat.

Opposite: *Rube Marquard was in the twilight of his 201-177 big-league career when he finally arrived in Brooklyn to toil during the 1916-1920 campaigns. Marquard would post a 56-48 record overall for Brooklyn and contribute 19 victories during the 1917 season.*

Above: *Slugging hero Zack Wheat crosses first base after legging out a 1926 base hit against the rival Giants at the Polo Grounds.*

Right: *Manager Robinson receives a good luck charm from his wife during pre-game festivities before the second contest of the 1920 Fall Classic.*

In the seasons which followed throughout the roaring twenties, two unbending marks of consistency character- ized National League play in Ebbets Field. Wilbert Robinson remained entrenched as manager and later as club presi- dent as well. And the Dodgers seemed to hold a long-term lease on sixth place. That is precisely where the ball club sat each and every season between 1922 and 1929 — with the brief exception of a second-place pennant run in 1924. In the midst of continual front-office upheaval during the final years of the McKeever family ownership of the Brooklyn ball club, Robbie proved remarkably adept at holding on to his job. At the same time his clubs proved nowhere near as adept at winning ball games.

The Robinson years did witness some of the most colorful and talented ballplayers to wear the Brooklyn uniform, as well as some of the most storied events of Brooklyn baseball lore. Zack Wheat amassed Brooklyn's longest playing career, hitting over .300 in 13 different seasons and en- joying two consecutive .375 seasons in 1923 and 1924. Nap Rucker toiled for weak-hitting Brooklyn teams between 1907 and 1916 and compiled an unimpressive lifetime mark of 134-134, but today he is considered perhaps the finest natural left-hander ever to pitch for Brooklyn. The hard- luck Rucker once won 22 games for a 1911 Brooklyn ball club which amassed only 64 season victories. Babe Herman was, for all his reputed defensive shortcomings, perhaps the finest natural hitter ever to pull on the Brooklyn colors, enjoying a remarkable 1930 campaign in which he batted .393 (an all-time franchise standard) and drove home 130 runs. Dazzy Vance and Burleigh Grimes provided Brooklyn with the league's most intimidating pitching duo of the 1920s, with Vance leading the league twice in games won and Grimes winning 20 on four different occasions.

It was ultimately the colorful exploits of the 1920s Dodgers as bumbling baseball showmen that most dis- tinguished the Wilbert Robinson chapter of Brooklyn base- ball history. Robinson was always dogged by unusual events. Most legendary perhaps is the 1926 debacle in Ebbets Field when headstrong Babe Herman ran a certain double into an unpredictable double play, a matchless and often retold moment that found three confused Dodgers simultaneously standing on third base. Equally bizarre was the moment when catcher Zack Taylor (the incident is often erroneously reported as involving Herman) legged out a triple and then stepped off the bag to receive the backslap- ping congratulations of his bemused manager, then coach- ing third, only to be tagged out in the process. Even visiting teams brought zaniness to Ebbets Field during Robinson's long tenure. Casey Stengel punctuated his celebrated 1918 return to Brooklyn in a Pittsburgh uniform by doffing his cap to the jeering crowd and releasing a captive sparrow tucked under his headgear. But Uncle Robbie had early set the tone for such highjinks among his Brooklyn charges when he attempted to catch a baseball dropped from a cir- cling biplane during spring training of 1916. The falling sphere turned out to be a grapefruit (supplied by the puck- ish Stengel), which splattered all over the startled ex- catcher, convincing him momentarily that his own head had been split open in the process.

The popular image of Brooklyn's Dodgers as bumbling buffoons stems largely from the final few seasons of Wilbert Robinson's lengthy Brooklyn career. These were the Depression-era seasons at the close of the 1920s and the outset of the 1930s, when an endless string of second- division finishes did little to enliven play in Brooklyn. And no figure of this period comes more consistently to mind

Opposite: *Dodger southpaw Sherrod Smith warms up to start in Game Three of the 1920 World Series with Cleveland's Indians. Smith would split two games yet compile a brilliant 0.53 ERA over 17 innings.*

Above right: *Robin Tommy Griffith slides into third during 1920 Series action.*

Right: *Aging Dazzy Vance was still the Robins' ace hurler in the 1928 season with an NL-best 2.09 ERA.*

than the redoubtable Babe Herman. Herman was an athlete of extraordinary talent when it came to hitting a baseball, yet history has not treated this Babe kindly when it comes to legendary baseball reputation. In one marvelous summer he tore apart the National League with a .393 average and 130 runs batted in. Yet though Herman later became a good defensive fielder he had been a bungling gloveman in his early career — hit squarely on the head more than once by an errant fly ball — plus an erratic base runner with a nose for disaster right down to his final major league campaign of 1945.

No incident of Herman's career better capsulizes the charm of the Daffy Dodgers than one that took place in Ebbets Field on a sleepy summer Sunday afternoon of 1926. Like much baseball legend, this incident has outgrown the original event. And the villain of the piece was, of course, Babe Herman, who managed to gallop into history as the star of perhaps the most inept moment of baserunning that the national game has ever produced. In the opening game of a doubleheader that day between two of the season's most dreary teams — Brooklyn and Boston — longtime third base coach Otto Miller and bench jockey catcher Mickey O'Neil decided to switch positions for an inning, perhaps simply to break an afternoon's boredom. On a team not known for discipline, manager Wilbert Robinson was neither informed of the switch nor attentive enough to notice it. But what happened next was enough to rivet Uncle Robbie's attention, as well as that of everyone else in the ballpark.

The score was tied 1-1 in the seventh and the bases filled with Dodgers. Babe Herman poked a towering fly to center and then tore around the bases as Boston outfielder Jimmy

Opposite: *Several Dodger outfielders (l to r) — Jigger Statz, Rube Bressler, Harvey Henrick, Ty Tyson, Babe Herman, and Max Carey — pose in a rare 1928 cameo. This was the first of Herman's three incredible years at the plate, seasons in which he hit .340, .381 and .390.*

Right: *Catcher Hank DeBerry (l) and ace hurler Dazzy Vance (r) here enjoy a light-hearted moment during Florida spring training.*

Below: *The Opening Day parade for the 1934 Brooklyn Dodgers inaugurates another "next year" at Ebbets Field. It would prove to be a long season for the faithful as rookie manager Casey Stengel led his club to yet another discouraging sixth-place finish.*

Welch chased down the prodigious blast while Dodgers runners stood their ground fearing a last-minute leaping catch. Once the ball bounced off the center field fence, Hank DeBerry scored from third, Dazzy Vance lumbered past third on his way to the plate as well, and Chick Fewster scrambled from first to third with Herman nipping at his heels.

It was then that Fate and the ineptitude of a novice third base coach conspired to write Herman forever into baseball lore. "Back! Back!" screamed the disoriented Mickey O'Neil from the coach's box, desperately trying to halt the charge of the reckless Herman. Yet it was the unpredictable Vance alone who heard the coach's pleas, sliding back into third where he was promptly greeted by the near simultaneous arrival of Fewster and Herman as well. Amazed Boston third sacker Eddie Taylor wasted little in tagging the confused Vance and Herman, now both standing on the bag; but somehow Taylor missed Fewster. Only Herman was out, of course, as Vance was entitled to the bag; but the inattentive Fewster assumed a double play and disgustedly departed for his own defensive position at second base. What then transpired was a genuinely comic scene, with Boston second baseman Doc Gautreau chasing the chagrined Fewster halfway around right field before managing to make the final hilarious putout.

What almost always goes unmentioned about this most amusing moment of all Dodgers history is the not insignificant fact that Herman's blast to center delivered the game's winning run in the person of DeBerry. But this was the kind of rare baseball moment from which folklore is born, and the actual events pale before the symbolic significance of Dodger baserunning ineptitude. Legend even has it that a passing cabbie, stuck in traffic outside the ballpark at that very moment, had shouted to fans at the top of the grandstand at the instant of the legendary incident, begging an explanation for the uproar from the packed stands. "We're losin' two to one, in the bottom of the eighth, but we got three men on base!" came the excited response from somewhere in the throng. "Which base?" shouted the dissatisfied cabbie — an ironically appropriate reply.

If Herman was an irrepressible ray of sunshine in Ebbets Field, there were few bright thunderbolts like him after the Babe was traded away to Cincinnati at the conclusion of the 1931 season. The early and middle years of the 1930s saw three successive star-crossed managers try vainly to lift the entertaining yet hapless Dodgers out of a decade of second-division doldrums. Max Carey (1932-1933), Casey Stengel (1934-1936), and Burleigh Grimes — old-time Ebbets Field hands all — took turns at trying to right a sinking ship, yet each met with similar frustrations and identical failures.

Of the hopeless three, Casey enjoyed the most productive campaign, a third place finish in 1932, nine games behind the Chicago Cubs. Neither Stengel nor Grimes, by contrast, posted a single winning ledger nor finished a summer higher than fifth place. Yet the standard for daffy play which had reached such heights under Wilbert Robinson also failed to slacken under Uncle Robbie's three immediate successors as well. Skipper Stengel in particular was blessed with a continuation of trademark Dodger daffiness to which Casey himself often contributed in ample measure, assisted by such memorable characters as outfielder Frenchy Bordagaray, streaky hitter Len Koenecke, and intemperate slugger Hack Wilson. Bordagaray — legend has it — once gave up on a routine fly ball against the Cubs merely to chase down his wind-blown cap in the outfield instead. Another cherished apocryphal incident involves the rotund Hack Wilson, here suffering through a gigantic hangover on a sunny afternoon in Philadelphia's Baker Bowl. Dodgers hurler Walter "Boom Boom" Beck, distraught about being removed from the mound that day by manager Stengel, refused to hand his skipper the ball and instead whirled and threw the offending sphere high against the right-field fence. Wilson, at that very moment lost in private thought while squinting at the grass before him, whirled suddenly, seized the caroming baseball, and threw a perfect strike to third base, well ahead of the phantom runner.

If manager Max Carey could at least savor smelling the first division once, and if manager Stengel at least managed to keep the Brooklyn tradition of daffiness alive, manager Grimes could boast of nothing but two seasons of abject ineptitude. The joyless departure of manager Grimes at the conclusion of the 1938 campaign ironically, it turns out, would soon unlatch the door to the long-awaited first decade of sustained baseball success in Brooklyn franchise history.

Opposite: *Debut manager Casey Stengel is all smiles during pre-game ceremonies before his first hours at the helm in Brooklyn on Opening Day of 1934. But Casey would be smiling far less as his three Brooklyn managerial seasons progressed.*

Above: *Young Hack Wilson takes a patent roundhouse cut during spring training action with the Giants in March 1925. A decade later the ill-fielding Wilson would be rounding out his short but spectacular career in a rival Brooklyn uniform.*

Right: *Giants skipper Bill Terry (l) and Bums pilot Burleigh Grimes enjoy the ceremonial handshake before the opening game of the 1937 league campaign. This was but three seasons after the unpopular Terry goaded Brooklyn fans with his gibe about Brooklyn still being in the league.*

3. HURRICANE LARRY CONSTRUCTS THE WARTIME DODGERS

No period of American history has known such unsettling upheavals and rapid transitions as the decade that encompassed World War II. Baseball also experienced its greatest turmoil and upheaval during this decade. The entry of the United States into the war in December 1941 meant the loss of the bulk of major leaguers to military conscription, as well as wartime travel restrictions and material shortages, which together impacted heavily upon the game. As war wound down across the globe, baseball encountered new manpower arrangements. The Mexican League made severe player-raiding forays into both the American and National leagues in 1946; ownership soon faced a nearly successful organization of the much-feared players' union; and by the close of the decade the major leagues had opened to both blacks and Hispanics. Air travel began to replace train travel as a means of ball club transport, and increased radio coverage of big league games was followed at the war's end with the first glimmers of televised baseball. Nighttime play, too, had become a well-established practice by the close of the decade.

In National League ballparks during this era two great ball clubs were also busy establishing their uncontested domination over the nation's favored sport of this new age. The St. Louis Cardinals, reaping the bounteous harvest of an elaborate farm system cultivated by Branch Rickey throughout the 1930s, captured four pennants and three World Series, while also finishing second five times between 1941 and 1949. In Brooklyn, a newly reconstructed Dodgers outfit, hastily put in place by innovative Larry MacPhail at the close of the previous decade, also emerged as a potent force, winning three pennants and grabbing three second-place finishes as well. Only 1945 (Cubs) and 1948 (Braves) saw anything but Cardinal and Dodger domination of the senior circuit during the remainder of the decade.

The primary authors of the success that swept Brooklyn baseball on the eve of the Second World War were an innovative general manager and the fireplug field manager who was to be his first and most remarkable front-office acquisition. Under pioneering front-office boss Larry Mac-Phail and dugout general Leo "The Lip" Durocher, the Dodgers wasted little time launching a decade of baseball triumphs that would end once and forever Brooklyn's long-standing image of impossible losers and incorrigible baseball clowns.

The long-awaited transition in Brooklyn baseball fortunes, however, did not come without considerable pressure from outside forces. Nearly a decade and a half of feuding over control of the organization, precipitated by Charles

Ebbets's sudden death in 1925, had left the Brooklyn franchise on the brink of destruction. By the close of the 1937 season, National League president Ford Frick, fearing the possible demise of one of the circuit's oldest and once most stable ball clubs, intervened and urged that Brooklyn ownership employ fresh blood to man the front office. Frick's nominee for the role was Leland Stanford MacPhail, a Branch Rickey protégé who had most recently run the Cincinnati club for Powel Crosley. MacPhail had amply established his front-office skills while running business for the Cincinnati ball club, turning around an almost moribund outfit in a few short seasons and pioneering such baseball firsts as major league night baseball and commercial radio broadcasting of Cincinnati home ball games.

MacPhail was quick to bring these same innovations to Brooklyn, employing his honey-voiced Cincinnati broadcaster Walter "Red" Barber to air the first games from Ebbets Field, and scheduling as well the first New York City night game at Ebbets Field in June of 1938. MacPhail — a genius for crowd-promoting gimmicks — also hired Babe Ruth as his Dodgers' nominal first base coach and batting instructor. While Ruth lasted only a single season in this demeaning role and was bitterly disappointed at not being considered for a managerial slot at the conclusion of 1938, his brief appearance in Brooklyn did bring hordes of fans out to the grandstand to watch him take batting practice and crush line drives onto nearby Bedford Avenue. MacPhail also occupied his first season in Brooklyn with acquiring hitting talent that would radically alter the course of Dodgers history within a few short seasons.

Batting star Dolf Camilli was first purchased from the Phillies for $50,000. Future fan-favorite Fred "Dixie" Walker was next obtained on waivers from the Tigers in July 1939. A young jewel from the St. Louis Cardinals' farm system, promising outfielder "Pistol Pete" Reiser, was plucked from free-agency (imposed by Commissioner Ford Frick in retribution for Branch Rickey's tainted farm system practices) for an almost laughable $100 bonus. Harold "Pee Wee" Reese was similarly stolen from the Boston Red Sox organization early in 1940, and slugging star Joe Medwick was acquired from the Cardinals the same summer. Medwick, however, was soon severely injured when beaned by St. Louis hurler Bob Bowman only a week after the trade and never proved the valuable outfield addition the Dodgers and MacPhail had coveted.

MacPhail was a breath of fresh air for Brooklyn (some poetic authors have termed him more a full-scale hurricane) and for all of New York and National League baseball. The new Dodgers boss spent several thousand dollars renovating Ebbets Field, painting and repairing the well-worn grandstand and refurbishing restrooms and clubhouse facilities. His decision to send home games out over the radio airwaves in 1938 was a stroke of genius. The move, which broke a long-standing gentlemen's agreement between the three New York ball clubs not to provide free radio access to locally played games, launched the age of regular radio baseball broadcasts in the nation's largest city

Opposite: *Two teams would dominate the wartime-era senior circuit — the club Branch Rickey had earlier built in St. Louis and the one he now constructed in Brooklyn. When the Cards and Dodgers met it was always a cause for rare excitement, demonstrated by these fans lining up for ducats to a 1942 Bums-Cardinals doubleheader.*

Above: *Ex-Dodger boss Larry MacPhail gets the lowdown from the new Mahatma, Branch Rickey.*

Right: *Popular Bums first sacker Dolf Camilli slides safely home against the Chicago Cubs in late-1940s Ebbets Field action. Clyde McCullough is the Cubbies catcher in this exciting game action.*

Above: *Rookie shortstop Reese was stolen from the Boston Red Sox in 1940.*

Below: *The first Ebbets Field night game in 1938.*

Right: *Pete Reiser slides safely across home plate with a pure reckless exuberance that marked his entire exciting, if injury-plagued, Brooklyn career.*

and largest media market. MacPhail's dismissal of former pitching ace Burleigh Grimes as manager and his simultaneous promotion of shortstop Leo Durocher to the bench for the opening of the 1939 campaign heralded a new era of Dodger successes beginning with a near 1940 pennant and the team's first league title in 21 seasons the following year.

But it was MacPhail's introduction of night baseball that provided the final highlight of the prewar decade. Fan response to the first Ebbets Field arc-light game on June 15, 1938, played against MacPhail's former club, the Cincinnati Reds, was so overwhelming that fire marshals had to close the gates several hours before game time. MacPhail's circus-like pre-game events included an exhibition footrace featuring recent Olympic hero Jesse Owens. Enhancing the special atmosphere of the evening was the fact that the Reds starting hurler, the young left-handed fastballer Johnny Vander Meer, was fresh off a masterful no-hit performance against the Boston Braves only four nights earlier. History was on MacPhail's side that night, and with a strong boost from Brooklyn's primitive illumination system, Vander Meer became the first and only pitcher in baseball history to pitch a second consecutive no-hit game. A new era of nighttime baseball had opened under MacPhail with perhaps the most famous game ever played in the 44-year history of storied Ebbets Field.

While the Dodgers were as decimated by wartime baseball as most of their league rivals, with Leo Durocher's arrival in Brooklyn a steady climb began toward the league's top rung. First there were two proud first-division finishes in 1939 and 1940. The Cincinnati ball club that MacPhail had earlier built was now the cream of the league, but the Cardinals and the upstart Dodgers stood ready and challenging in the wings.

The summer of 1941 is now best remembered for the feats of two American League sluggers. New York's Joe DiMaggio fashioned a memorable hitting streak which today remains baseball's most romanticized milestone, while Boston's Ted Williams was on his way to becoming the last of a dying breed — the .400 hitter. But it was the Dodgers who authored more baseball excitement that summer than any other team in either league. A big part of that excitement was the play of youngster Pete Reiser. Another inspired dimension was the hard-nosed and often nasty play instilled in the Dodgers by Durocher. The season was crammed from first to last with brawls, feuds, spikings, and even bitter beanball wars. Quickly the Dodgers were becoming the most hated team in the senior circuit. But this was also a ball club that the Brooklyn partisans now dearly loved. Camilli led the circuit in homers and ribbies and was league MVP; Reiser led in most other offensive categories (doubles, triples, runs scored, total bases, slugging average, and batting); and by the end of the September Brooklyn itself led the league.

The World Series of 1941 was another story, however. Sure the Dodgers were finally in the Fall Classic after 21 seasons of lonely waiting. But what took place during the next week was an unfortunately grim harbinger of things to come — and to come repeatedly over the final two decades of Dodger residence in Ebbets Field. For that autumn witnessed the very worst of many painful moments that mark Brooklyn's baseball history. The opponent was an impressive — perhaps invincible — Yankee ball club that was in the midst of capturing seven pennants in eight years. But in the end the Brooklyn team seemed to beat itself, and do it largely in one inexcusable moment of defensive collapse.

No long-time Dodgers fan will ever forget what happened

on October 5, 1941, almost exactly a decade before Bobby Thomson and the "shot heard round the world." For many a hardy Brooklyn soul, that day in 1941 ranks in infamy even above the day in which Thomson robbed the Bums of a certain pennant. After three hard-fought contests the powerhouse Yankees led by the slimmest of margins – two games to one – and the Dodgers seemed poised to knot the Series. With Hugh Casey hurling strong relief, Durocher's men entered the ninth frame leading 4-3. With two already retired and victory a single pitch away Yankee stalwart Tommy Henrich waved helplessly at a wicked Casey curve for the game-ending third strike. But wait! The ball skipped past an unprepared catcher, Mickey Owen, and rolled disastrously to the backstop while Henrich pranced to first. Three hits and a walk later and the game and Series were both hopelessly lost.

By 1946 the Dodgers, like their rivals, were again at full strength. Postwar return of veterans meant a team that blended experienced hands with rookie hopefuls. The familiar faces included Reese at shortstop, Lavagetto and Reiser in the outfield, and Casey and Higbie throwing from the mound. But the summer's genuine surprise was a rifle-

armed rookie outfielder named Carl Furillo. In his first big league season, Furillo hit .284. He also established a reputation around the league for a cannon right arm which could gun down opposing base runners with rare regularity. With Reiser and Furillo chasing flies and Reese anchoring the infield, the Dodgers were back in business.

The end result was that the Brooklyn Dodgers were soon once more enjoying a dogfight pennant race with the rival St. Louis Cardinals. The Dodgers would lead by seven games in mid-July, then fade badly down the stretch and allow the Cardinals to catch them on the league's final day. It would be the first post-season tie-breaker playoff in baseball history, and the best-of-three mini-series that followed would be all St. Louis. Howie Pollet's complete-game masterpiece bested Ralph Branca in the opener; an 8-1 rout quickly settled the closer. The Dodgers thus were more lopsided losers to the Cardinals in 1946 than they would be when they faced the Giants in yet another infamous playoff five years down the road. But in the first season of the new optimistic postwar era, the Brooklyn inclination toward unrelenting daffiness was already being replaced with an equal penchant for unrelieved late-season disaster.

Left: *For a moment in Game One of the 1941 World Series Brooklyn catcher Mickey Owen seemed destined for a hero's role with this fifth-inning triple at Yankee Stadium. Owen slides dramatically into third as Reese scores ahead of him with the first Brooklyn Series run. The lead would not stand, however, and Owen would himself soon enough be trading in victor's roses for loser's hemlock.*

Opposite above: *Cookie Lavagetto scores for Brooklyn in bang-bang home plate action during the seventh inning of the 1941 opening Series contest. Bill Dickey is the Yankee catcher and the crouching number 8 for Brooklyn is on-deck batter Dixie Walker.*

Below: *Four days later Mickey Owen would be involved in a more famous and far more ominous moment of Brooklyn World Series history. The snakebit Brooklyn catcher takes off in pursuit of Hugh Casey's unexpected spitball delivery which has just whizzed past Yankee Tommy Henrich for the potential game-ending strikeout, but also eludes Owen in the most infamous botched moment in Dodgers history. Owen's passed ball would allow a Yankee rally which put Brooklyn behind three games to one and closed the door on the first of many World Series defeats at the hands of the Series-charmed New York Yankees.*

Overleaf: *Durocher's 1942 Brooklyn club won four more games than the league champion 1941 outfit. Yet the first Dodgers ball club of the wartime years was doomed to finish a tight second, two games behind the pitching-rich Cardinals. Those relentless Cardinals charged back from a 10-game deficit in August.*

Dodgers
Dodgers
Dodgers
Dodgers
Dodgers
Dodgers
Dodgers
Dodgers
Dodgers
Dodgers
Dodgers
Dodgers
Dodgers
Dodgers

4. JACK BE NIMBLE, JACK BE QUICK!

Perhaps no chapter in baseball history is more romanticized than the story of Jackie Robinson's pioneering role in breaking baseball's long-standing and inexcusable racial barriers. It has now been 45 summers since Robinson and Branch Rickey shook the post-World War II baseball community to its foundations. No previous or subsequent event in the history of the national pastime has had such far-reaching impact.

Certainly no single event has more dramatically shaped baseball's future course. Not Babe Ruth's shattering feat of 59 and then 60 homers in a single season; not the Black Sox scandal that wrecked the 1919 Cincinnati-Chicago World Series and nearly brought down the reputation of the nation's favored sport; not the exciting and much bally-hooed chase of Ty Cobb's immortal career hitting mark by the beloved "Charlie Hustle," Pete Rose; and not "the streak" of Joltin' Joe DiMaggio, which lasted 56 games and then withstood all challenges for over a half century. The introduction of a reputed lively ball in the early 1920s (or at least the legislation of a spotlessly clean ball for each and

Left: *Jackie Robinson signs autographs for adoring youngsters before a final pre-season game on April 10, 1947. A day later Robbie would make his historic National League debut in Ebbets Field.*

Opposite top: *Jackie Robinson inks his 1949 Dodgers contract in the presence of Brooklyn club president Branch Rickey (r) and field manager Burt Shotton (l), thus paving the way for Jackie's spectacular MVP third big league season.*

Opposite bottom: *Robinson slides safely into second base in Game One of the 1947 World Series in Yankee Stadium, successfully outlegging the throw to Yankee shortstop Phil Rizzuto. Jackie would bang out seven hits, score three runs and steal two bases during his rookie World Series appearance.*

every pitch, alongside the invention of a lively swinging style by Ruth and his imitators) shifted the balance from pitching to hitting in a way that put tens of thousands of new fans into the grandstands. Nighttime baseball brought another new wave of fans, as did television at the close of World War II and West Coast expansion a decade later. But nothing impacted on baseball — indeed saved the game, with a timely infusion of both justice and untapped player talent — as did the ending of that embarrassing "gentlemen's agreement" that had long kept America's treasured national institution as lily white as the horsehide ball itself.

Jackie Robinson's remarkable and controversial debut had such impact that Red Barber later referred to the season that housed it as "the year all hell broke loose in baseball." The precise moment of this occasion was the early afternoon of April 15, 1947, when a 28-year-old rookie opened the season in Ebbets Field as the starting Brooklyn first baseman and thus in a flash became the first recognized black player to appear in a 20th-century major league game. With his debut against the Boston Braves that day, Jackie Robinson put a ringing end to an odious baseball tradition that had been firmly implanted since Cap Anson and his cronies had deemed all blacks unwelcome on white-dominated big league or minor league ball fields as far back as the close of the 1880s.

Today, of course, it is easy to view Robinson's debut somewhat differently against the backdrop of history. Blacks are now prominent in most professional sports. And these many years after the hoopla of Rickey's bold experiment we know that Robinson was not, technically speaking, the first black player of the modern-era 20th century. Not, at least, if one admits the ancestry of several pioneering Latin American players who made cameo big league appearances in the decades preceding Robinson. Two Cubans, for example, played with the Washington Senators three full decades earlier; outfielder Jacinto "Jack" Calvo took his cuts in 33 games in 1913 and later in 1920, while hurler Jose Acosta won 10 games in the combined seasons of 1920-22 with the Nats and the Chicago White Sox. These men were dark-skinned enough to be fully accepted as black athletes by the Negro League teams for which they also played. Another Cuban pitcher with ebony skin-tone anticipated Robinson as well, by only three seasons. Tommy de la Cruz was treated with hostility and misgivings by the Reds fans and was dropped by Cincinnati management at the end of a single 1944 season. None of this lessens the impact of Robinson's debut at the time it happened.

Robinson's appearance in the big leagues had not come about overnight. Visionary Brooklyn club president and general manager Branch Rickey had long been tormented by the discriminatory policies of the professional sport to which he had devoted his own life. Devoutly religious as well as schooled in the shrewdest of business practices, Rickey had burned over an incident he had suffered as a collegiate coach in 1904: one of Rickey's star players, a black named Charlie Thomas, had been reportedly reduced to tears of frustration when denied a room in the team hotel. But as much as he was stung by such injustice, Rickey, who developed the modern farm system, was also keenly aware that the time had come in the wake of World War II to open a new untapped font of available baseball talent. He had surreptitiously scouted Robinson while the latter played with the Negro League Kansas City Monarchs and considered him the perfect man for a master plan to integrate baseball. As the story has often been told, Rickey needed an extraordinary athlete of contradictory and even paradoxical personality; a man of burning competitive spirit who would not quit under the severest pressures, yet also a man who would never strike back in justified anger at the most outrageous personal and racial insults. Robinson ultimately became Rickey's man.

During the remainder of that first season and throughout all of the next, Jackie Robinson faced the loneliest of personal battles. Few in management or on the field were as

Above left: *A multi-sport star on the UCLA campus, Jackie Robinson here wins the long jump competition in a May 1940 meet at the LA Coliseum. As winner of the 1940 NCAA long jump title, Jackie would undoubtedly have competed in the 1940 Olympic Games had not war brought cancellation of the prestigious event.*

Above right: *Robinson also starred as a triple-threat back for the UCLA Bruins football squad, averaging over 11 yards per carry as a fleet-footed halfback during his junior season. Robbie even led Pacific Coast Conference teams in basketball scoring during both his junior and senior years on campus.*

Left: *The youthful Robbie here poses with Rickey's special assistant Robert Finch during workouts of the Montreal Royals farm team in Sanford, Florida. The season is 1946.*

Opposite top: *Robinson crosses home plate after hitting a circuit blast in his debut AAA game with the Montreal Royals.*

willing as Rickey to concede the inherent unfairness or moral injustice of baseball's policy toward the nation's black citizens. Many of Robbie's own teammates were cut from just such bigoted cloth. Despite a spectacular minor league season one summer earlier in Montreal, Robinson was hardly welcomed into the Brooklyn clubhouse. Popular outfielder Dixie "The Peeple's Cherce" Walker, a 1944 league batting champion, was traded away to the Pittsburgh Pirates at the end of the 1947 season precisely because of his outspoken opposition to playing on the same ball club as Robinson. Yet there were some teammates who quickly realized – in light of an embarrassing post-season pennant loss to the Cardinals the previous fall – that this rookie could well put victories on the board and thus dollars in their shallow pockets. Robinson was soon making easy converts of his pliable bench mates with a National League Rookie of the Year campaign, a .297 batting average, a team-high 29 stolen bases, and an irrepressible flashy style of daring offensive and defensive play.

Yet if fans and club mates in Brooklyn were quickly won over, such was not the case throughout the rest of the league. Merciless jeering from fans and opponents, ceaseless bench-jockeying from opposing managers, vicious hate mail, and even death threats followed Robinson and the Brooklyn ball club around the senior circuit throughout the 1947 and 1948 league campaigns. Usually mild-mannered NL president Ford Frick even fired off an angry warning of wholesale suspensions when the St. Louis and Philadelphia franchises threatened at the outset to boycott games against the Brooklyn ball club.

Recent research by two of baseball's most astute scholars has revealed that Rickey's original plan was not exactly the one that unfolded. Historians John Thorn and Jules Tygiel have uncovered evidence that Rickey indeed planned to sign several black players simultaneously in the autumn of 1945. Robinson was not intended to carry the burden of pioneering alone. But fate had a different plan. Persistent rumors about the "Old Mahatma's" impending integration plan eventually forced Rickey's hand, and Robinson's signing to a Montreal Royals contract had to be announced

before a more ambitious multi-player signing could be orchestrated.

It is also clear in the hindsight of history that Rickey's motives in bringing blacks into organized baseball were not precisely as legend would now have them. Rickey undoubtedly was driven by a sincere sense of larger mission. But it is clear, as well, that the astute big league executive also wanted desperately to win ball games, and his long-planned exploitation of a new source of baseball talent was soon being justified by a continued attack in the press on what he saw as the exploitive nature of the Negro Leagues themselves. In the end, Rickey's plan was as devastating to the institution of black professional baseball as it was fruitful for talent-hungry major league clubs. In effect Rickey killed off the Negro Leagues by robbing their limited talent base with no provision for compensation to Negro League club owners.

Yet whatever the impact of Rickey's experiment on black baseball, the impact in Brooklyn remains unquestioned, for the birth of Jackie Robinson's career in the National League was also the birth of the modern-day Brooklyn Dodgers. The team rode joyously upon the wings of Robinson's spectacular rookie season as it soared through the National League schedule. And the 1947 World Series that followed (a rematch of the fateful 1941 match-up with the crosstown Yankees) was one of the most action-packed Fall Classics of all time. It was also one of the strangest; one of those rare Series encounters when unheralded journeymen like Floyd Bevens, Al Gionfriddo, and Cookie Lavagetto would unexpectedly rise to outshine more established stars like DiMaggio, Robinson, Reese, and Berra. Bevens missed World Series immortality by the narrowest margin; Lavagetto turned Bevens's near-masterpiece into his own moment of glory; and Gionfriddo made a circus catch unrivaled until a man named Amoros. And then, as if in payment for their brush with destiny, all three disappeared forever from major league lineups as soon as the curtain rang down on the final Series putout.

It was the 1947 Series that witnessed the most memorable base hit in Brooklyn Dodgers history. The setting was

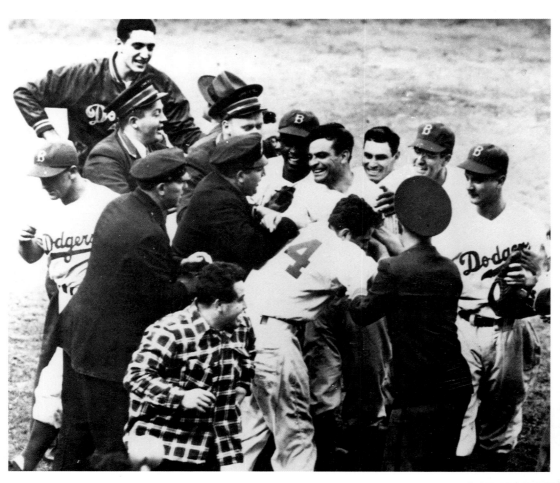

Left: *The celebration begins as Cookie Lavagetto has just ruined Bill Bevens's 1947 shot at a no-hitter and World Series immortality.*

Below: *Jackie Robinson is welcomed to the Brooklyn dugout by his big league teammates in April 1947.*

Opposite top: *Brooklyn hurler Preacher Roe enjoys a rare base-running moment as he outlegs a belated throw to Cubs first sacker Phil Cavaretta during a mid-season 1949 contest.*

Opposite bottom: *Jackie Robinson and Don Newcombe enjoy a friendly pre-game moment with commissioner Happy Chandler just prior to Game One of the 1949 Series. Newcombe would suffer a heartbreaking loss that afternoon as Henrich's ninth-inning solo homer would beat him 1-0.*

Game Four, as pitcher Floyd Bevens flirted that day with a rare kind of immortality at the expense of the often-victimized Dodgers. By the eighth inning Bevens was clearly on his way to an unprecedented World Series no-hitter. In the ninth inning, however, Cookie Lavagetto etched his name forever in loyal Brooklyn hearts with a ringing base hit that not only broke Bevens's spell but stole the game from New York as well. Lavagetto's timely hit, Gionfriddo's memorable Game Six catch, and even Hugh Casey's rebound from 1941 Series disaster with six appearances and a subterranean 0.87 ERA — none were enough in the end to prevent a seven-game New York Series triumph.

The 1949 season found Robinson and the Dodgers back in the forefront of the hunt after a slight tumble in 1948. And it was in this season that Jackie Robinson would also enjoy his best year — a league-leading .342 average, 37 stolen bases, 12 triples, 124 ribbies. The World Series of 1949 would be packed full of its own share of unduplicated thrills. Having assumed the backstop duties, Roy Campanella would begin a string of five Fall Classics in which he would catch every inning. New Yankee skipper Casey Stengel launched his own run of five straight world titles. And again the Yankees were victors, this time easy victors. Yet the Dodgers had clearly arrived and the future seemed to hold no limits for the team that Branch Rickey had built around his trio of black stars — Robinson, Campanella, and fireballing hurler Don Newcombe.

Ironically neither of Brooklyn's two great integration heroes would last long in the limelight of the New York baseball scene. Jackie would flash his reckless playing style for only a handful of seasons longer. And Branch Rickey was destined to depart even sooner. Increasingly uncomfortable with rival partner Walter O'Malley, Rickey would sell out his club interests and depart for another challenging rebuilding job in Pittsburgh by 1950. Yet whatever else might be said about these two fiery competitors in the afterglow of history, Rickey and Robinson had unquestionably radically changed the face of tradition-rich baseball forever.

5. THE DUKE OF FLATBUSH

Throughout most of the 1950s, they were a baseball team that held the hearts of the racially and ethnically mixed borough of Brooklyn. Later, with an assist from author Roger Kahn, their reputation for colorful play and their penchant for late-hour traumatic defeats captured a full nation of baseball fans. These were the Dodgers of the last decade of baseball in Brooklyn – Campanella, Snider, Robinson, Reese, Erskine, Furillo, Hodges, Cox, Gilliam, Newcombe, Black, Shuba. This was an awesome team, which dominated the National League for most of a full decade. Yet it was a fate-wracked team as well, more noble in our rose-tinted memories for their tragic eleventh-hour defeats on closing days of consecutive seasons and in the annual Subway Series with the hated rival Yankees than for their relentless domination of baseball's senior circuit.

To live in or around New York in the mid-1950s was to enjoy a feast of some of the most colorful hometown baseball stars ever assembled in one location for such a succession of summers. Mantle and Berra paraded their wares with the Yankees; Willie Mays and Monte Irvin flashed in the outfield for the tradition-rich Giants. But the fullest roster of individual heroes seemed always to wear the historic flannels of the Dodgers. It was this alone that made their regular World Series defeats each autumn seem so utterly incomprehensible.

Four slugging heroes above all others reigned in sprawling Brooklyn. Their presence loomed so large that even the irrepressible Jackie Robinson was inevitably reduced to second-billing. Rotund Roy Campanella was the most brilliant backstop of his era, overshadowing even the dangerous and colorful Yogi Berra everywhere except perhaps among the most intractable Yankee diehards. Pee Wee Reese had no parallel among shortstops in either league. He

Below: *Reese and Robinson practice their famed double-play relay during 1957 spring practice.*

Opposite: *Roy Campanella tosses his mask sky high as he goes after a foul pop at Ebbets Field.*

Above left: *Gil Hodges, the slugging first sacker, in a 1952 pose.*

Above right: *Duke Snider swings from the heels in an oft-seen 1949 portrait.*

Opposite: *Snider practices his trademark of plucking and chewing a blade of the outfield pasture, here during a moment of 1953 World Series action.*

was the man of many enigmatic nicknames: "Pee Wee" resulting not from physical stature but from childhood skill as a marble shooter; "The Little Colonel" reflecting his days as star shortstop for the American Association Louisville Colonels; "The Captain" pointing to his much deserved stature as field leader of a big-league ball club that won seven pennants under his field leadership. It was Pee Wee who remained the most warmly regarded Dodger among Brooklyn baseball stalwarts – 35,000 partisans once turning out for a 1955 Ebbets Field birthday party to shower their star with $20,000 in gifts, lighting candles and singing "Happy Birthday" to serenade their cherished hero between innings of a league game. Gil Hodges was also a force at first base with no parallel in either league. He was a gentle giant in the mold of Gehrig who earned such respect from hometown fans that they stood and cheered his every appearance even during a dreadful 0-for-21 1952 World Series tailspin. Today Gil Hodges remains the most mysterious oversight in the history of Hall-of-Fame balloting. And looming even larger than the rest was slugger Duke Snider, the most glamorous Brooklyn Dodger of them all.

Of course, in some respects Edwin "Duke" Snider was simply not cut from the right cloth to be a Dodgers stalwart of the same order as Campanella, Reese, or Hodges. For one thing, Snider stood apart from his team and his community, a troublesome paradox and an endless mystery. Here was a graceful fly chaser who often sulked about personal batting slumps and loafed on routine defensive plays – a commonplace, perhaps, among 1990s high-salaried sports

stars but a true rarity during baseball's radio age. But there was also something magical about Duke Snider that, for a short spell at least, made him the most magnetic baseball figure in a city unrivaled as the baseball capital of the world.

For one thing, no big league ballplayer ever sported a better nickname, one that seemed to guarantee a slugging Hall-of-Fame career and baseball immortality. But the "Duke of Flatbush" was as much victim as beneficiary of his glowing press clippings, for his potential was seemingly so great that no matter what his achievements on the field, he seemed always to fall somehow short – for fans and the media alike – of his expected greatness.

Certainly no major league star ever played more directly in the glare of publicity. Baseball was the unchallenged king of sports in New York City during the decade of the 1950s, and each of that city's three great teams boasted a future Hall-of-Famer performing in center field. With Mickey Mantle pacing the Yankees and Willie Mays thrilling Giants fans, Duke Snider often seemed to be only the third best outfielder playing in the nation's baseball capital. It didn't help that newspaper accounts flowing from spring training in 1947 and 1948 promoted the untried young

Dodger outfielder as the "new Stan Musial" and a certainty to be the greatest Brooklyn sensation ever. With that kind of buildup, it seemed that the Duke would be a major disappointment no matter what he did once he reached Ebbets Field.

Mantle was the darling of an effusive New York press corps and was adopted by newspaper writers and fans as the heir to the great Yankee tradition of Babe Ruth and Joe DiMaggio. Mickey therefore had the most difficult task of the three in living up to the standards set by Yankee heroes of past eras. After all, Ruth, Gehrig, and DiMaggio were already a central part of the country's baseball mythology. Mays, on the other hand, earned instant fame with his seemingly impossible 1954 World Series catch of a towering fly ball off the bat of Vic Wertz. The catch was witnessed by a television audience of millions and thus made Willie an instant national folk hero. Mays also emerged during the years of the mid-fifties as a rare phenomenon — a powerful slugger with awesome speed and considerable defensive flair. He would be blessed with a productive career of 22 full seasons that far outstretched his two rivals, extending his lofty credentials as time marched on and first Snider and later Mantle faded from the scene.

Duke, at the same time, was the undisputed champion of all Brooklyn. For the thousands of Dodgers faithful there was always the feeling that the Duke never quite got his fair judgment from the New York baseball writers, just as the entire Brooklyn borough never seemed to get a fair shake when compared with sophisticated Manhattan or the teeming Bronx. The press was captivated by an idea that people

from Brooklyn simply talked funny and were rough and ready blue-collar sorts, and the sports pages fell in love with an image of Snider as a sulker and an unreasonably moody ball player. Yet one of those Brooklyn diehards still remembered years later that "Mays made just that one catch in the World Series. But for day-in, day-out baseball, Snider was the best. Snider was simply spectacular!"

In the early going Duke Snider did have clear flaws as a big-league hitter. While he showed almost unlimited potential with his outfield speed and potent throwing arm and with his graceful long-ball swing, the Duke was clearly an undisciplined hitter who struck out at a record pace. And when he struck out he often sulked and fretted, which then affected his play in the field as well. Snider's moodiness may have been exaggerated by sportswriters in the Big Apple and around the nation, but there was some truth to the charge.

The master teacher Branch Rickey had a plan, however, to salvage his promising rookie outfielder. When the Old Mahatma had first released statements to the press calling Snider "the jewel of the organization" and the "man with the perfect swing," he was perhaps only trying to divert attention away from his 1947 noble experiment with Jackie Robinson and the smashing of baseball's color line. But his praise of Snider was also genuine, based on a belief that the young man was headed for stardom. Now he simply had to teach him to master big-league pitchers. During spring training of 1948, with the Robinson experiment accomplished, Rickey pressed the Snider reclamation project into effect by assigning Hall-of-Famer George Sisler to work with

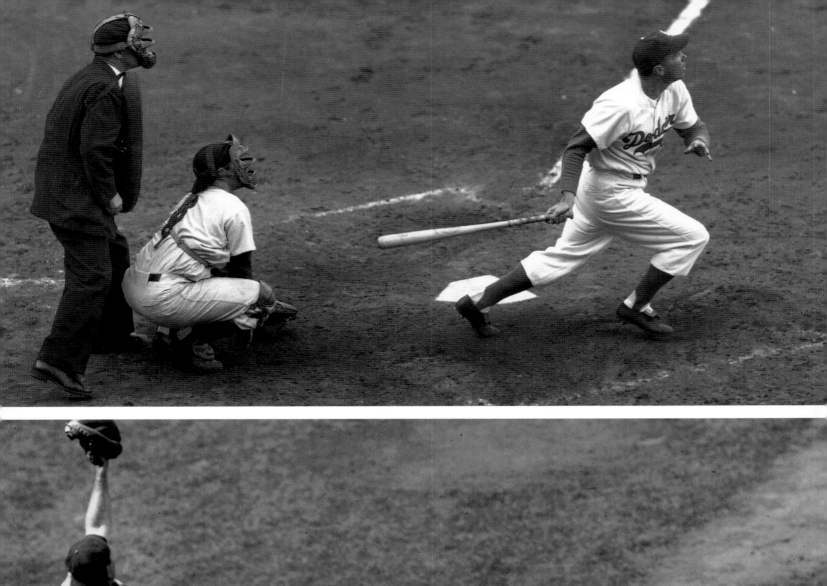

Opposite top: *All eyes look skyward as umpire, batter and catcher watch the flight of Snider's mammoth circuit blast, his second during Game Six of the 1952 World Series.*

Opposite bottom: *The Duke slides safely home as Cubs catcher Mickey Owen, of 1941 World Series fame, leaps for the errant throw during 1950 Ebbets Field game action.*

Right: *Duke Snider displays three balls representing his three homers during the 1950 Memorial Day Dodgers-Phillies doubleheader. Skipper Burt Shotton looks on approvingly.*

Duke as a private batting tutor. The two veteran teachers were hard taskmasters with their undisciplined pupil. Snider was made to stand in the batter's box with his bat on his shoulder, watching and calling each of hundreds of pitches for Mr. Rickey. In this way Duke would learn the strike zone and also learn the secret of waiting on a pitch. When discipline finally came to his batting, only then could Snider become the great hitter that Rickey and the Dodgers hoped for.

Strikeouts would remain a major problem throughout Snider's career. Three times the Duke would exceed all league hitters in this category, and three times as well during the Brooklyn years his season's whiff total would equal or surpass his number for runs batted in. But after his sessions with Rickey and Sisler, the free-swinger had been molded into an awesome big-league slugger. Duke hated to strike out and sometimes he worried too much about not hitting safely every time up to the plate. But after 1950, the Duke was taking plenty of revenge against the league's pitchers who had caused him so many headaches on his first few trips around the circuit.

For a few seasons in the early 1950s, Duke Snider was hurt not only by his own over-anxiousness at the plate, but also by his own team's failure to live up to the standards of the rival Yankees and Giants. Never did these team failures glare so disturbingly as in the disappointing 1950 season and the 1951 pennant race that followed it. Never in baseball history had a powerhouse team been so snake-bitten by fickle fortune for two seasons in a row.

First came the loss of a pennant on the final day of the 1950 season, as Brooklyn was edged out by the surprising Philadelphia Phillies when Dick Sisler smacked a dramatic extra-inning home run. Fate had treated the Brooklyn ball club and their star center fielder unkindly that day. With the game tied and the season's pennant on the line, Snider stroked a ninth-inning single that seemed to send Cal Abrams home from second with the deciding run. But in an infamous moment of Brooklyn bungling, Abrams inexplicably stumbled rounding third and Philadelphia outfielder Rickie Ashburn nailed him with a perfect throw to the plate. Duke Snider could just as well have been the celebrated hero of that 1950 campaign, but glory was robbed from him

by Abrams's fateful stumble and Ashburn's miraculous throw.

Soon came yet another even more momentous late-season collapse during the closing days of September 1951. While the Dodgers and Phillies had battled neck and neck all summer long in 1950 as they raced toward their dramatic final weekend pennant showdown, the 1951 season seemed destined to be a Brooklyn runaway until the final weeks. But by then Durocher's Giants had won 16 of their final 20 to close a five-and-a-half game Brooklyn lead and force the National League's second-ever post-season playoff series.

Events of the final Dodgers-Giants playoff game of October 1951 have been told over and over again. The "Miracle at Coogan's Bluff" is among the most widely discussed single moments of the nation's sporting history. It is estimated that three million or more family television sets were tuned to the championship contest that day, and Bobby Thomson's dramatic game-ending ninth-inning homer was perhaps the nation's first major sporting moment viewed live by a national audience. For generations of ball fans the vivid image has remained intact of Thomson rounding third and heading for a mob scene of waiting teammates at home plate, manager Durocher leaping in hot pursuit from the third base coaching box, dejected Dodger hurler Ralph Branca — ominous number 13 in full view on his uniform back — strolling forlornly to the distant Brooklyn clubhouse in deepest center field.

Again the Duke might have been a hero of the pennant race and World Series that year, but again he was left standing unrewarded on the sidelines. Bobby Thomson's fateful blow soon came to be known as "the shot heard round the world." Mantle and Mays would play only small roles in the 1951 Series that fall, but they were now already part of a winning tradition. It seemed as if Snider and his Dodgers, for all their mid-season heroics, were destined to be annual losers when post-season championship play rolled around.

But from 1953 through 1957 Duke Snider of Brooklyn led not only Mays and Mantle but all other rivals by a wide margin when it came to regular-season offensive numbers. There were three straight summers over the stretch when Duke topped the senior circuit in runs scored. In 1955 he was the RBI leader and the following summer he paced the

Above: *The most famous home run in all baseball history has just left the bat of Bobby Thomson during the ninth inning of the final Dodgers-Giants playoff game on October 3, 1951.*

Left: *Thomson is mobbed by teammates and spectators at home plate moments later, while dejected hurler Ralph Branca departs the mound and Brooklyn infielder Jackie Robinson (42) stands stunned at second base.*

Opposite: *Duke Snider and journeyman infielder Tommy Brown provide hitting tips to Florida little leaguers at the Dodgers' 1951 Vero Beach training camp.*

circuit in homers as well. Four straight years he knocked in over 100 runs and scored 100 or more as well. And in 1957, Snider tied Ralph Kiner's league mark by hitting 40 homers or better for the fifth season running. Duke also had many great individual days, and none was greater than the afternoon when he slugged three Ebbets Field homers and barely missed a fourth (a double high off the right field wall) against the Philadelphia Phillies ball club.

As Duke's reputation mounted steadily on the field, a stormy relationship blossomed with the Ebbets Field fans and the Brooklyn baseball press. Two incidents stood at the center of that relationship. The first came when Snider blasted the fans for booing him and his teammates after a tough Dodger loss. "These are the worst fans in baseball," he stormed to reporters in the locker room, "and you can print that." The next day a huge headline carrying Duke's words appeared which was certain to stir strong emotions among the ballpark faithful. Snider reported to Ebbets Field that next night prepared for the worst and was soon getting it. By the end of the game, however, after he banged out a long homer and two doubles, the fans were once again cheering him wildly. Brooklyn fans were hotheaded and emotional, just like the Duke himself, but they were also most forgiving of their cherished heroes.

A second Snider run-in with the fans was not quite so quickly forgiven. Duke had been pressed for an interview by writer Roger Kahn at the close of Brooklyn's successful 1955 championship season and had agreed finally to speak freely about his career-long frustrations with baseball. In May 1956 the article appeared in *Collier's* magazine with the headline "I Play Baseball for Money — Not Fun, by Duke Snider." Duke complained sincerely in that article that life in the big leagues was a tiresome and serious business and not the endless picnic that most fans imagined. Once the story appeared, Snider was again the focal point of strong emotions and considerable criticism. Newspapers around the country blasted him for his abandonment of baseball as

an ideal dreamworld. The Duke, of course, felt he had been largely misunderstood. But he swallowed his pride and quietly went back about the business of hitting homers and winning ball games.

Throughout the early 1950s Duke Snider continued to team with his old rookie roommate Gil Hodges to form one of the great one-two hitting punches in the major leagues. Few righty-lefty power combos have been more destructive of enemy pitching. For 15 seasons the potent pair played together in Dodgers uniforms and continued to assault league hurlers for a total of 745 home runs. In the end Snider and Hodges would form the third best homer combination in National League annals. Only Aaron and Mathews, alongside Mays and McCovey, would ever top them. And if American Leaguers were added to the tally, only Babe Ruth and the Duke's boyhood hero Lou Gehrig — playing together for the Murderers' Row Yankees of the 1920s and 1930s — ever formed a more devastating long-ball pair.

Despite all the long-ball bashing that took place in Ebbets Field during those glorious years, however, the Brooklyn franchise remained hobbled by fate. Even the wrecking crew ball clubs of the 1940s and 1950s — those managed by Shotton, Dressen, and Alston, and starring such Cooperstown immortals as Jackie Robinson, Roy Campanella, Duke Snider, and Pee Wee Reese — were unable to escape totally the "lovable losers" image that plagued Brooklyn teams right down to their final seasons in Ebbets Field. While dominating the National League thoroughly during the decade from the end of World War II until the dawn of baseball's western expansion, these Dodgers seemed always to be merely fodder for the cannons of those unbeatable "Damn Yankees" when baseball's October Classic rolled around. This may well have been one of baseball's most talented outfits during that brilliant ballpark epoch of the 1950s, but it was also only the second best team in the city of New York!

Left: *Carl Erskine was the most steady moundsman of the "Boys of Summer," a double-figure winner six straight summers and author of two no-hitters.*

Below: *These were the "Boys of Summer" in their glorious prime – Snider, Hodges, Campanella, and Furillo (l to r). This lumber accounted for 135 homers in 1953 and 120 more in 1954.*

Opposite: *Ralph Branca will always live in the collective memories of Dodgers fans for a single fateful pitch to Bobby Thomson in October 1951. Yet Branca, winner of 21 games in 1947, was a fine hurler of considerable accomplishment.*

6. "THE BOYS OF SUMMER"

Writer Roger Kahn immortalized them as "The Boys of Summer" and they have become one of the most famous teams in baseball history. The outfits occupying Ebbets Field during the early and mid-1950s were plagued from the first with an undeserved reputation as hopeless losers. They were, after all, only the second best team in New York City. The Brooklyn ball club of that era is today best remembered as yearly losers to the powerful New York Yankees of puckish manager Casey Stengel, perennial victims in what became known to the rest of the nation as the annual "Subway Series" between the Yankees and Dodgers to decide baseball's world champion. Between 1947 and 1956 these two teams met six times in World Series play, and only once could Brooklyn muster a Series win. Five times the Brooklyn Bums were disappointing World Series victims of the champion Yankees paced by Yogi Berra, Whitey Ford, and Mickey Mantle. Twice more this same Brooklyn ball club saw pennant dreams and golden opportunities to play in two additional World Series slip from their grasp in the final inning of play on the very last day of the season. While the Yankees reigned invincible season after season, the cry for Brooklyn fans was always "Wait until next year!"

But like so much else in baseball, Kahn's image of the Brooklyn Dodgers as hopeless "also-rans" is more myth than substance. The actual record shows that this was the most dominant team in National League history. A third-place finish in 1948 (seven and a half games behind Boston) represents the only summer of 11 (1946-1956) that the Dodgers were not serious contenders into the season's final week. Victories on the final day of the campaign in 1946, 1950, and 1951 would have given Brooklyn an unheard-of nine pennants in 11 seasons, and only 19 more victories (less than two a year) between 1946 and 1956 would have resulted in an unimaginable 11 straight National League flags. Even the Yankees never managed that kind of total league domination.

This was also one of the most colorful, star-studded teams in the history of National League baseball. Duke Snider, Roy Campanella, Gil Hodges, Pee Wee Reese, Jackie Robinson, Don Newcombe, Carl Erskine, Preacher Roe, Sal

Maglie — the lineup card reads like an all-time, all-star dream team, not an actual batting order to be sent on to the field each day for most of a decade. The roster included four future Hall-of-Famers, four additional perennial all-stars, and some of the best defensive stars in the game, as well, in the persons of third sacker Billy Cox, second baseman Junior Gilliam, and shotgun-arm right fielder Carl Furillo.

It was only pitching, perhaps, that seemed to fail the Bums in their regular annual autumn showdowns with the power-laden Yankees. The Brooklyn bullpen was admittedly strong. While the now popular "save" did not become an officially sanctioned statistical category until 1969, a perusal of reconstructed save counts in the *Baseball Encyclopedia* today reveals that Dodger relievers like Labine, Branca, Palica, Roebuck, Loes, and Jim Hughes often ranked among senior circuit leaders. Hugh Casey was an early Brooklyn pacesetter of the era, topping the unofficial National League list with 18 in 1947, while Joe Black was a single-season contender during his exceptional rookie campaign of 1952. Hughes paced the circuit with 24 in 1954, Roebuck and Labine together finished second and third in 1955, and Labine stood atop the league's heap with 19 in 1956 and 17 in 1957. Yet starting hurlers like Don Newcombe, Preacher Roe, and Duke Snider's valued roommate, Carl Erskine, while they were adequate for a season of National League competition, were clearly no match for the lustrous Yankee staff of Whitey Ford, Allie Reynolds, Vic Raschi, and Eddie Lopat during annual post-season match-ups.

Offense, on the other hand, was the Dodgers' strong suit. The slugging trio of Snider, Campanella, and Hodges hit 100 or more homers for five straight years. Dodger hitters accounted for two league batting titles (Robinson in 1949 and Furillo in 1953), one home run title (Snider in 1956), two RBI leaderships (Campanella in 1953 and Snider in 1955), and four stolen base championships (Reiser in 1946, Robinson in 1947 and 1949, Reese in 1952). If the Yankees owned the baseball world for the full decade after World War II, the Brooklyn Dodgers certainly owned the National League.

Brooklyn's reputation for spectacular losing was built on more than the dramatic pennant collapses of 1950 and 1951, of course. There were also memorable defeats in back-to-back World Series match-ups of 1952 and 1953, Series that might well have been won with a single well-timed hit or two, or perhaps a little better pitching when the chips were down. The 1952 Series is perhaps best remembered today for the failures of slugging first baseman Gil Hodges who, despite 32 homers and 102 RBIs in regular season play, could not muster even a single hit in 21 Series at-bats against superior Yankee pitching. The hopeful Dodgers had won the first, third, and fifth games, including two of three games played at Yankee Stadium. But the Yankees roared back with two final victories in Ebbets Field, sending the ill-fated Dodgers to their sixth straight World Series defeat.

The final two games on the familiar turf of Ebbets Field were tightly contested and turned on almost every pitch. But Mantle hit a clutch homer to seal Brooklyn's fate in Game Six. And it was the most unlikely of heroes who did in the hometown Bums in Game Seven. Mantle had again homered and singled to establish a New York lead and then expand it. Yet in the home seventh the Dodgers had loaded the bases with but a single out. Snider failed with a pop out, however, and then Robinson also hit a towering infield pop fly. It was on Robinson's ball that feisty infielder Billy Martin charged across the diamond to make a near-impossible one-handed grab that sent the Dodgers packing with another Series defeat. Martin was the kind of unsung last-minute hero that the Yankees always seemed to find and the Dodgers always seemed somehow to lack.

Opposite: *1952 NL Champs – a club which would hold a 3-2 Series lead before losing two straight in Ebbets Field.*

Below: *Carl Erskine whiffs Yankees' Gil McDougald en route to a record 14 strikeouts in Game Three of the 1953 World Series.*

Opposite top left: In a 1987 survey of former big leaguers Jackie Robinson was labeled the greatest of his era at second base, yet the pioneering Robinson broke into the majors as a first sacker, since Eddie Stanky won the Brooklyn second base slot at the time.

Opposite top right: Roy Campanella captured three league MVP honors in five seasons, yet his career was also slowed by injury and ended prematurely by a fateful auto accident. Roy hit with power and fielded with grace, yet his true contribution may have been his handling of the Bums' impressive mound staff.

Opposite bottom left: Carl Furillo was a cannon in right field, and 30 years later they still marvel at what may have been the finest outfield throwing arm the game has ever seen.

Opposite bottom right: Big Don Newcombe anchored the mound staff from early April to the closing weeks of September, yet he could never quite live down a reputation for repeated World Series failures.

Right: Duke Snider was never a darling of the New York press like Mantle, nor the rage of latter-day baseball historians like Mays, yet in Brooklyn during the 1950s the Duke was a unanimous choice as the greatest player who ever lived.

Duke Snider alone blasted four homers during the 1952 Fall Classic – a record-tying effort – but it simply wasn't enough. The 1953 Series saw more of the same, this time a four-to-two margin for Stengel's Yankees, despite the rebound Series play of Gil Hodges with a .364 average, a Brooklyn team batting average of .300 for the entire Series, and another homer and four RBIs by the dependable Duke Snider in the Dodgers' final victory of Game Four. This time the Dodgers were dead-even after four games. But once again the Yankees charged away at the wire, sweeping Game Five 11-7 and then eking out a Game Six 4-3 nail-biter. Ironically, it was again the pesky Billy Martin who did in the Dodgers. Martin, batting .500 for the entire Series, singled home the tie-breaking run in the bottom of the ninth to bring the New York Yankees their fifth straight World Championship.

Duke Snider never had a better stage for his awesome slugging talents than that provided by each autumn's renewal of World Series play. For four special seasons (1952-53 and 1955-56) the Fall Classic seemed to be Duke's own personal showcase. It was true that the Dodgers rarely won the annual autumn showdown with the Yankees, but Snider never had to take a back seat during October to his own personal rival, Mickey Mantle. While Mickey poked 8 homers and knocked home 17 runs in these four head-to-head Series match-ups, Duke slugged 10 roundtrippers and accounted for a whopping 24 RBIs of his own.

It was the bookend Series matchups of 1952 and 1953 that truly launched Snider's period of World Series mastery. Duke's .345 batting average in 1952 was nearly duplicated with his .320 mark in 1953. Mantle also batted .345 in the first of these back-to-back Subway Series, but then fell off to a lackluster .208 in the second. The debate might rage on about the best center fielder in New York during the summer months, but Snider was winning hands down for the honor of best in autumn Series play.

The summer of 1954 provided a rare off-season for the Brooklyn Dodgers. But it certainly wasn't the hitting that

Left: *Gil Hodges displays the ball blasted for his 200th career homer, the first Dodger to reach this milestone figure.*

Opposite top: *Campanella registers a homeplate putout of Billy Martin during Game Four of the 1953 World Series.*

Opposite bottom: *Snider displays his graceful outfield play with a spectacular grab in the 1953 World Series.*

Overleaf: *The 1955 World Champion Brooklyn Dodgers, the only Bums outfit in 67 seasons that didn't have to "wait 'til next year!"*

could be faulted – a league-best .444 slugging average, the league's top homer total, and second best in the circuit in team batting. For Duke Snider, in particular, it was a truly great year, perhaps the finest of his exceptional career. Snider's batting average zoomed to .341, only four points behind Mays for the league batting championship. He tied teammate Hodges for second in the senior circuit in RBIs with 130 and stood second overall in base hits as well. In slugging average only Mays was better. For that one season, at least, the question about who was the champion slugging center fielder in the baseball capital of New York was restricted to the National Leaguers – Mays versus Snider.

But if Duke Snider owned National League pitchers in 1954, for his Brooklyn ball club it was seemingly just another year of gigantic collapse. Willie Mays was back from two years of military service and his refreshed Giants ran off with the league crown as Brooklyn slumped five games behind under unheralded rookie manager Walter Alston. It was beginning to appear as if the glory years might have passed Duke and his teammates by without a single championship crown. It truly seemed as though the beloved Bums were never going to find a way to win it all for themselves and for the legions of rabid local partisans.

The Dodgers edition of 1954 may have seen disappointments, but the 1955 ball club was far from a defeated bunch. A new leader had now been found, as Snider inherited the symbolic role from the aging Jackie Robinson and the fading Pee Wee Reese. On the heels of his marvelous 1954 slugging campaign, Duke Snider was also about to generate even greater fireworks with his most productive overall year ever. Buoyed by Snider's slugging, the Dodgers shot from the starting gate with a league-record opening 10-game win streak and then posted 22 triumphs in their first 24 contests. By the end of April the Bums held an incredible nine-game lead over second-place Milwaukee and would never look back for the remainder of the runaway season. It looked as though the old blood coursing through the collective veins of the "Boys of Summer" was not quite exhausted.

It was soon evident that 1955 would at last be the Bums' long-awaited "next year." When it finally happened, nothing was more responsible than Duke Snider's solo performance in the Fall Classic that once again unfolded against those crosstown Yankees. It was the fifth Subway Series in eight years and this one was destined to be one of the most dramatic. This would be a Series later remembered by baseball's fans and historians as the one in which youthful lefty Johnny Podres pitched two sterling victorious games and unheralded Cuban Sandy Amoros made a marvelous catch in the sixth inning of the final game (turning an apparent Berra extra-base hit into a rally-quenching double play) to preserve Brooklyn's first World Championship ever. Yet Snider was once again the man who provided almost all the heavy artillery.

Throughout the Series Snider hit, ran, and threw as he had never done before. The Duke played like a man possessed. His long-ball blasts in Games Four and Five provided the needed victory margins that set the stage for Brooklyn's championship. Duke ripped four homers in that Series and thus became the only man ever to sock four Series roundtrippers for the second time during a career. The Dodgers were now baseball's champions for the first time in their 65-year history, and they were the first team ever to come back and win a Series after dropping the opening two games. Equally satisfying was the fact that Duke Snider's heroic World Series slugging had at last proven indispensable to a Dodgers' victory.

Yet if Brooklyn waited the better part of a century to savor World Championship victory, the Bums would not have long to enjoy their new status. The post-championship summer of 1956 would be a bittersweet last hurrah for this rapidly aging Brooklyn ball club that had dominated the senior circuit for much of a full decade. The summer certainly did not start as though the club had any notion of collapsing. A still-solid Brooklyn lineup managed to hold tenaciously to a slim lead over an improved Milwaukee outfit and surprise Cincinnati contingent for a narrow pennant victory that found all three clubs bunched in a two-game span by season's close.

The World Series of 1956 was a distinct disappointment, however. If 1955 had finally brought glory for Brooklyn, the 1956 renewal of the Subway Series demonstrated that it was back to business as usual. Once again the Yankees

would dominate the Dodgers, just as they had for a painfully long decade. But this time the embarrassments seemed even grander in scale. An opening two-game lead fashioned in Ebbets Field quickly evaporated in Yankee Stadium. A hurler named Don Larsen stole the Series spotlight by victimizing Brooklyn hitters with the only perfect game of Fall Classic history, and a deciding seventh game in Brooklyn provided a nightmarish slaughter as Yankee bats pounded Series goat Don Newcombe for five runs in three innings on the way to a 9-0 clincher. As brilliant as Newcombe was summer-in and summer-out, against the Yankees he seemed little more than yearly cannon fodder.

Although no one quite knew it at the time, with the final pitch of the 1956 Fall Classic the curtain had wrung down not only on a championship series and yet another season, but also on a fast-fading baseball era and a cherished ball club as well. The Dodgers days in Brooklyn were now limited and ebbing fast. The first sign would be the painful departure of Jackie Robinson, the very symbol of Brooklyn baseball during the postwar period. Sold to the rival Giants for $35,000 in a surprising off-season move, Robinson immediately announced his retirement rather than don any uniform other than that of the Brooklyn nine. Now 38 and aged beyond his years, he had little speed or reflexes left.

Other signs were there for those who would see them. Walter O'Malley had been sending strong signals for more than a year that he was no longer committed to keeping National League baseball in New York. Perhaps it was the stigma of trailing the Yankees at the gate, in the press, and at the championship wire, season after season. Perhaps there was something substantial to O'Malley's complaints about attendance at Ebbets Field. The park was now an aging relic and the rival Braves had been routinely shattering Dodgers attendance records ever since their own relocation to Milwaukee several season earlier. And perhaps O'Malley did see untold riches awaiting in California. Certainly he was frustrated in his efforts to get city officials to listen to modernization plans for a Brooklyn ball park. The Gotham City politicians were clearly as guilty of apathy as

the Brooklyn owner was of avarice. Although several sites for a new park on downtown Brooklyn Avenue adjacent to Atlantic Avenue were repeatedly suggested to government officials, the city simply refused to act.

If Brooklyn was on the verge of losing a baseball team in 1957, its fans seemed only aware of losing a pennant. The announcement in May that senior circuit owners had already sanctioned West Coast relocation of the Dodgers and Giants if only Walter O'Malley and Horace Stoneham would request it was greeted with little more than a collective yawn. The Brooklyn ball club slumped throughout the summer, attendance slumped further. Young pitchers named Drysdale and Koufax failed to stir much enthusiasm at the dawn of their promising careers, and the last edition of the Brooklyn Bums were never seriously in the hunt as they limped home a distant third behind the Braves and the pesky Cardinals. The worst news would not come until October, of course — a month in which Brooklyn had been conditioned to bad news by season after season of World Series disaster. On October 8th, as another World Series wound down in Yankee Stadium, O'Malley accepted a deal that would end Brooklyn baseball forever.

Once beyond the friendly confines of Ebbets Field, one by one the brightest of the old Dodgers lights flickered out. It is true that after a single disastrous season the new O'Malley team would rise from the ashes and reclaim a position atop the National League standings. And in the coming summers a new dynasty would be built. New Dodgers heroes would perform on a new stage for new fans. But these were never the Dodgers of old. Only two years after leaving Ebbets Field, names like Koufax, Drysdale, Neal, Howard, and Roseboro had replaced Erskine, Newcombe, Robinson, Snider, Reese, and Campanella. The old fire was gone. Perhaps with the coming of television, West Coast play, and domed and carpeted ballparks, it was baseball itself that had changed. The Dodgers were still a potent ball club — a very good championship ball club — but no longer a cherished social institution. "Dem Bums" were now a very distant memory.

Opposite: *The greatest moment of Brooklyn baseball history as Bums storm the field to celebrate a World Series title on October 4, 1955.*

Right: *Joyous Dodgers celebrate the Brooklyn World Series triumph – (l to r) Duke Snider, league president Warren Giles, Walter O'Malley, Johnny Podres and Gil Hodges.*

Below: *President Dwight Eisenhower tosses out the ceremonial first ball to open the 1956 Fall Classic. Also present are commissioner Ford Frick and managers Casey Stengel and Walter Alston of the rival Yankees and Dodgers.*

Opposite: *Veteran Preacher Roe (l) and youngster Johnny Podres discuss pitching strategy during a quiet spring training moment. Preacher Roe, left-handed ace of the Dodgers' staff between 1948 and 1954 won 93 and lost only 37 for Brooklyn. Admitting openly that he threw an illegal spitter, which along with crafty changes of speed made him one of the toughest NL hurlers of the 1950s, Roe twice led the circuit in winning percentage. Owning one of the best lifetime percentage marks (.627) in baseball history, Roe hung up his glove in 1955, just one season before Brooklyn, behind Podres, would finally win it all.*

Right: *Johnny Podres strikes the classic mound pose with which he mowed down Yankee batters in the final game of the 1955 World Series. In one brilliant Series outing the young Podres seemed to singlehandedly wash away the failures of Branca, Hugh Casey and Newcombe, whitewashing the Yankees in a crucial seventh-game matchup and thus bringing the Bums a first and only World Series crown.*

7. GALLERY OF BUMS ENTRENCHED IN COOPERSTOWN

Baseball is a game of endless mythic potential – a spectacle of breathing legends and heroic deeds. The timely home run blow of unsung Bobby Thomson, the circus catch of Willie Mays, the prodigious home run blasts of Babe Ruth are the stuff of pure nostalgia, much of it summoned with the names and faces of our ball player heroes. Baseball's constant interplay of pregnant pause and frenetic action creates time for reflection and thus for indelible memories. Its field of play is spread openly in full view so that each action and each athlete-turned-actor stands uncomplicated, clearly displayed, before us.

No team boasts a collection of more colorful and legendary heroes than the Dodgers who performed for half a century before the fans of Brooklyn. Each distinct age of the game in the first half of the 20th century has its honor roll of Dodger greats who rank among baseball's immortals. Some such as Casey Stengel, Babe Herman, and Leo Durocher were often zany clowns whose infamous deeds and riotous pranks marked the Brooklyn franchise with its lasting reputation for baseball color. Others, most certainly Jackie Robinson, Pete Reiser, and even Duke Snider are more truly tragic figures whose stories reflect baseball's marriage to both

Left: *It was not until 1959, 20 years after the establishment of baseball's lasting monument in Cooperstown and 33 seasons after his own career ended, that the Old Timers Committee recognized Zack Wheat with enshrinement as one of the game's immortals. Wheat was 70 at the time and residing in Sun Rise Beach, Missouri. But for those who saw him play, here was the greatest Dodger slugger of them all before Snider, and as popular as any player of his era in baseball-crazy New York — even including the legendary Babe Ruth.*

Opposite top: *Wheat's finest all-around year came during the Robins' pennant-winning campaign of 1916, a summer when he hit .312 and pulled off a 29-game batting streak.*

Opposite bottom: *Zack Wheat's only National League batting title was something of a bizarre footnote to baseball history, coming in the war-shortened 1918 campaign and resulting as much from front-office executive ruling as from events on the field.*

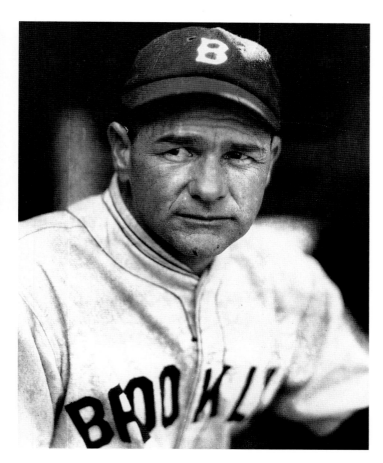

compiled in Mobile. Ebbets himself was skeptical at first, but eventually the desperate club president went along with Sutton's recommendations and purchased the untouted rookie from the South Association ball club for a hefty $1200. Wheat was an almost instant star upon arrival in Brooklyn, slugging for a .304 mark in his brief 26-game appearance of 1909, and then pounding rival pitching for a remarkable .317 lifetime average over the next 17 seasons spent in batter-friendly Ebbets Field. Registering 18 full seasons in the grey flannels of the Brooklyn Robins, Wheat also established an all-time longevity mark for Brooklyn players which still stands today, as do his team career milestones in games played (2322), at-bats (8859), hits (2804), doubles (464), triples (171), and total bases (4003). And all this from a player whose big-league career came to an end with a one-year stint for the Philadelphia Athletics over six decades ago, in the year that Babe Ruth smashed his record 60 home runs and Charles Lindbergh recorded his historic solo transatlantic flight.

Wheat's finest all-around performance came during the Robins' pennant-winning 1916 campaign, a year during which he hit .312 and ran off a 29-game batting streak, which was eventually stopped by Cincinnati's Fred Toney. Wheat's single National League batting title was something of a bizarre footnote to early baseball history, however, coming in the war-shortened campaign of 1918 and resulting as much from front-office executive ruling as from the events of on-field play. Brooklyn's stalwart was awarded the crown for his .335 average (compiled over 105 games) only when

luck and fate. A larger portion of Dodgers than with almost any other team have been elected to baseball's most select circle, enshrined in the game's archives, the Hall of Fame at Cooperstown.

Any complete history of the Dodgers, then, is in part a review of the careers and special achievements of a distinguished dozen or so of the game's giants – men who wore Brooklyn blue during the glory years of their major league careers. Such a review must begin with several forgotten heroes of an era long before baseball moved west, when the Brooklyn National League franchise was one of the league's most hopeless losers.

One unsung hero for the Brooklyn baseball club under Charles Ebbets at the turn of the century was ironically not a card-carrying baseball man at all. In one of his many strokes of intuitional genius, the young Ebbets, engaged an itinerant printer and spare-time ballpark vagabond, Larry Sutton, to serve as the club's single official talent scout. Scouting in the days before radio baseball was far removed from the glamorous endeavor it now appears to be in this age of computer and airplane. Scouts were solitary men who roamed the backwaters of bush-league baseball searching for the rare promising rube with enough talent to dazzle in the big time. And Sutton, for all his lack of formal baseball experience, seemed to have the most uncanny eye for such raw diamond talent. His stockpile of signees eventually included such Brooklyn standouts as Casey Stengel and Jake Daubert, along with hurlers Jeff Pfeffer and Sherrod Smith, fine second baseman George Cutshaw, and longtime catcher Otto Miller. But nowhere did Sutton strike the mother lode as he did in 1908 with the discovery of Zachariah Davis Wheat, a half part Missouri Cherokee who stood 5'10" and weighed but 170, when Brooklyn's free-wheeling scout stumbled upon him in the bush leagues at Mobile.

Wheat (dubbed Zack by most fans, but known as Buck to his teammates) possessed remarkable strength within his wiry frame, and the probing eye of Larry Sutton immediately saw an imposing left-handed batter of potential far beyond the anemic .246 average Wheat had recently

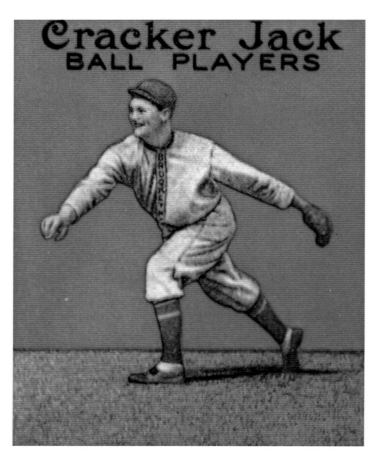

with developing the considerable pitching talents of Hall of Famer Rube Marquard), and finally as long-reigning manager for Brooklyn from 1914 until 1931.

Uncle Robbie's years in Brooklyn were mostly sanguine, if not always enlivened by winning baseball, at least as long as Charles Ebbets was alive. Yet after the sudden death of Ebbets in 1925 Robinson was increasingly caught in the ceaseless cross fire of vicious infighting between Steve McKeever and the Ebbets family as they wrestled for control of the Brooklyn franchise. Robbie even became compromise president of the ball club at the time of Ebbets's departure, a position that he occupied concurrent with his managerial role, yet one which quickly proved impossible in the long run. Later years of his Brooklyn tenure were marred by increasingly strained relationships with McKeever, hostile dealings with the sportswriters who always befuddled the nearly illiterate manager, and constant buffoonery on the part of his players, who repeatedly took advantage of his excessive good nature and of the always relaxed atmosphere

Left: *Zack Wheat's rare and colorful 1914 Cracker Jack collectors' card.*

Below: *Brooklyn manager Wilbert Robinson.*

Opposite: *"Uncle Robbie" strikes a jovial fatherly managerial pose during a 1927 photo session in Ebbets Field.*

Billy Southworth of Pittsburgh (.341 in 64 games) was declared ineligible for insufficient at-bats in a controversial ruling by league president John Heydler. Yet despite his scarcity of league hitting titles and pennant-winning clubs, Zack Wheat must be declared the first true superstar of modern-era Brooklyn baseball. In the mid-1920s, for example, while Ruth was socking record homers for the Yankees and Frankie Frisch was sparking the rival Giants, Wheat was surprisingly voted "most popular ballplayer" from the entire metropolis of New York in a newspaper poll taken among the always knowledgeable Gotham baseball fans.

Zack Wheat's lengthy career spanned two decades now fondly remembered in Brooklyn baseball lore as the era of one of New York's most colorful sporting legends, Wilbert Robinson. "Uncle Robbie" (to players and fans alike during his 18-year managerial and front-office tenure) was indeed legendary in his own time. While successful enough as a talented catcher for John McGraw's powerhouse National League Baltimore Orioles of the 1890s, he is best remembered as a Falstaffian figure of considerable baseball acumen who presided season after season over an outmanned roster of hopeless losers in Brooklyn. The team that bore his name (Robins) finished fifth or worse in six of seven seasons during one spell (relieved only by the pennant run of 1916), then recorded seven sixth-place records in eight years (somehow surprisingly jumping to second in 1924) during another. The popular conception of Uncle Robbie was always that of an amiable leader cursed with less than enthusiastic players. His teams almost always seemed short on talent but often long on tomfoolery and boneheaded play. Wilbert Robinson, in fact, was perhaps the perfect prototype for Durocher's later admonition that "nice guys finish last."

But while Robinson justly deserved some of his widespread reputation for lunacy, his baseball skills were also considerable, first as standout catcher with the Orioles (where he once went seven-for-seven and drove in 11 runs in a single ball game in 1892), later as John McGraw's confidant and coach with the Giants (where he was credited

in the Brooklyn clubhouse. Removed as president in 1929 and finally as manager in 1931, Uncle Robbie left his lengthy residence in Brooklyn with only two pennants salvaged from two decades of largely incompetent play. Few figures in Brooklyn baseball have loomed as large as Wilbert Robinson, however, and if it were not for the remarkable modern-day Los Angeles career of Walter Alston, Robbie would still hold the longest tenure of any Dodger manager in the club's 106-year history.

Uncle Robbie's tenure in Flatbush was not entirely without players of considerable skill. Pitchers in particular graced Brooklyn in this epoch with some remarkable baseball talent. None was more terrifying a prospect for opposing batters than powerful right-hander Burleigh Grimes, a mainstay of the Brooklyn mound corps between 1918 and 1926. Over this nine-year period Grimes posted victory totals of 19 (1918), 23 (1920), 22 (1921), 17 (1922), 21 (1923), and 22 (1924), amassing a laudable 158-121 record under Robinson and posting club standards which still stand for single season shutouts (seven in 1918) and earned runs allowed (138 in 1925). The latter marks, in particular, suggest that while Grimes was immensely talented, he was obviously not blessed with an outstanding supporting cast during his final Brooklyn years.

A distinguishing feature of Burleigh Grimes from the outset was a league-wide reputation for sullenness, along with a temper and disposition as mean as his feared fastball. Grimes feuded with teammates and opponents alike (he never spoke with Uncle Robbie for several seasons, so great was their acrimony), and he sported a reputation among the league's batsmen as an altogether frightening hurler to face. Old Stubblebeard won 270 games in his 19-year big-league career, and of the 17 established spitball pitchers allowed to continue their trade when "wet ones" were outlawed in 1920, Grimes hung around the longest, still serving them up until his final season with the Cardinals, Pirates, and Yankees in 1934. He wore a cap one size too small for his melon-shaped head and sported a stubble-growth beard to enhance his fearsome appearance. Right down to his swan-song 1934 season Grimes continued terrifying all the league's best hitters with knockdowns and dustoffs, aimed at stars like Bill Terry or Frankie Frisch, or at raw rookies like Cubs novice Art Weiss, with equal malice and with little detectable discrimination.

Yet for all his fearsome fastballing, Burleigh Grimes was only the second best right-hander of which the Robins could boast in those dry-spell years of the 1920s. Ace of the Brooklyn staff was fellow Hall of Famer Arthur C. "Dazzy" Vance, arguably the best right-handed moundsman in Brooklyn baseball history. Dazzy Vance reigned as National League strikeout king a remarkable seven seasons between 1922 and 1928 (three more than Koufax in the 1960s). He

won league MVP honors after his remarkable 1924 summer (28-6, .824), a year in which Rogers Hornsby had batted a modern-day record of .424 for the season but could not catch Vance in the MVP voting. Vance was also National League ERA champion on three different occasions, remarkably in seasons when his teammates finished second (1924), sixth (1928), and fourth (1930). Indeed, it is the single greatest testimony to the pitching mastery of Vance and Grimes that they posted a 355-261 record between them during a decade when Robbie's boys consistently finished well into the second division. Vance's own total of 190 victories established an all-time career standard not surpassed by pitchers wearing the Brooklyn uniform. He remains the third winningest all-time Dodger, trailing only Los Angeles hurlers Don Drysdale and Don Sutton.

If Grimes was mean and deceptive, living by the brushback pitch and the spitter, Vance was blinding speed. His career total 2045 strikeouts (1918 with Brooklyn) was a stratospheric figure in the decades before Feller, Koufax, and Nolan Ryan. But Dazzy's career surprisingly had a less-than-auspicious start, and his successes in Brooklyn, like those of Zack Wheat a decade earlier, were unanticipated and unlikely. A minor league vagabond for over a decade before World War I, Vance came to the Robins when the minor league New Orleans Pelicans insisted Brooklyn take the luckless pitcher as part of a deal for coveted catcher Hank DeBerry. Joining Uncle Robbie's boys in the spring of 1922, Vance didn't win his first big-league game until the hoary age of 31, yet compiled 196 more in the 15-year career that followed. No subsequent big leaguer has won so many victories after starting a career so late, and this was a point about which Dazzy Vance proudly boasted years later during his own Cooperstown induction in the summer of 1955.

When it comes to the modern-age Dodgers — Dodgers teams of the post-Depression era — there is perhaps only a single hands-down candidate for such accolades as "most colorful," "most daring," "most reckless," or "most inspired." Jackie Robinson constructed a legendary Hall of Fame career that can never be measured by raw numbers catalogued within the *Baseball Encyclopedia*, or by the yardsticks and minutiae faithfully applied by baseball's ever-prevalent statistics. A brilliantly gifted athlete who had excelled in three sports at UCLA before launching his professional baseball career with the Negro League Kansas City Monarchs, Robinson played only 10 seasons once he reached the big leagues. It must be remembered, when viewing Robinson's career totals, that his passage into the

Above: *Burleigh Grimes warms up in Cleveland for his starting assignment in Game Five of the 1920 World Series. Of 17 established spitballers allowed to continue their trade after wet ones were outlawed in 1920, "Old Stubblebeard" would hang around for the longest tenure.*

Right: *Future Cooperstown resident Dazzy Vance strikes a classic hurling pose at the Robins' spring training camp. The late-blooming Vance was the dominant strikeout pitcher of the National League during the 1920s, pacing the circuit seven straight times in this category.*

majors had been delayed until well after his 28th birthday. It should also be noted that Brooklyn won six pennants, finishing second on three occasions and third once during the decade spanned by Robinson's career.

Today the name "Robinson" does not even appear on most Dodgers' lists of career batting statistics, his highest post on any such list being seventh in all-time runs scored (947). Perhaps the most exciting base stealer of all time, Robinson played in an age when the steal was given diminished role in the game — especially on a power-packed roster like that of the 1950s Dodgers — and his career total of 197 stolen bases belies his true speed and daring on the base paths. All this is to say that Jackie Robinson's impact on Dodger fortunes was genuinely incalculable. Yet Robinson did at the same time achieve a remarkable list of distinctions and awards for so brief a career — the major league's first Rookie of the Year in 1947, National League MVP and batting champion (.342) in 1949, stolen-base leader for the senior circuit in 1947 (29) and 1949 (37), and a yearly All-Star selection between 1949 and 1954. A line-drive hitter with a .311 lifetime average and the speed and on-base percentage of a leadoff man, Robinson smashed 137 homers and often batted cleanup for managers Leo Durocher and Charlie Dressen as well.

The full gripping account of Robinson's racial integration of baseball — both its bitter disappointments and glorious triumphs — is rehearsed throughout baseball literature and provides subject matter for other chapters of this volume as well. The social pioneering of the great athlete has sometimes unfortunately shaded his true prowess on the ball field, for as a big league player, regardless of race or color, Robinson genuinely earned his Hall of Fame credentials by skilled and consistent performance alone. Robinson's highest achievements also had to do mostly with his unparalleled abilities — not often recorded in box scores and thus not subject to quantification — to turn around ball games in dramatic fashion and to beat opponents by guile and intimidation. Jackie repeatedly taunted and unnerved oppos-

JACK ROOSEVELT ROBINSON

BROOKLYN N.L. 1947 TO 1956
LEADING N.L. BATTER IN 1949. HOLDS FIELDING MARK FOR SECOND BASEMAN PLAYING IN 150 OR MORE GAMES WITH .992. LEAD N.L. IN STOLEN BASES IN 1947 AND 1949. MOST VALUABLE PLAYER IN 1949. LIFETIME BATTING AVERAGE .311. JOINT RECORD HOLDER FOR MOST DOUBLE PLAYS BY SECOND BASEMAN, 137 IN 1951. LED SECOND BASEMEN IN DOUBLE PLAYS 1949-50-51-52.

Opposite: *Jackie Robinson poses in Ebbets Field during the 1949 season, his finest big league campaign. It was in his third full campaign that Robbie would pace the league in BA and stolen bases, hit a career-high .342, and pace Brooklyn to a decade's third World Series showdown with the crosstown New York Yankees.*

Top right: *Robinson's Hall-of-Fame plaque lists impressive credentials, yet fails to capture the magnitude of Jackie's true impact on the nation's favored pastime.*

Bottom right: *Robinson poses with a number of earlier trophies after winning his greatest prize of all — National League MVP honors in 1949.*

Left: *Rookie catcher Roy Campanella strikes a fearsome batting pose during his maiden 1948 season. Campanella would catch only 78 games as major league baseball's first black receiver in 1948, but for the next 10 years he would remain the game's most durable and dependable backstop.*

Opposite: *Brooklyn's slugging backstop of the "Boys of Summer" era graphically demonstrates the "vicious" swing with which he would terrorize senior circuit hurlers for a full decade. This action is from the 1953 campaign, the second of Roy's three league MVP summers and a season in which he cracked 41 homers and a Brooklyn club record and league-best 142 RBIs.*

ing pitchers from the base paths. His daring baserunning feats and antics produced numerous unearned runs by aggravating and frustrating opposing infielders into frequent costly mistakes. And those who actually saw it will righteously contend that a Jackie Robinson steal of home was a thing of true beauty—perhaps the most thrilling sight in baseball.

Teammate Roy Campanella was also a pioneer in the racial integration of baseball, yet a less flashy ball player and a less forceful personality who always moved quietly within Robinson's giant shadow. It was a position that Campy never begrudged, perhaps even relished. While Robinson burned with smoldering fire, Campanella exuded good humor on and off the field and spoke baseball thunder with his reckless bat alone. In a career no longer than Robinson's (Campy reached Brooklyn a year later and played his last season the summer after Robinson's retirement) and cut off in its prime by a tragic automobile wreck, Campanella bashed 242 career homers (third on the all-time Dodger list), established the Brooklyn single-season RBI standard in 1953 with 142, and earned three National League MVP selections (1951, 1953, 1955). The latter was a feat duplicated only by Stan Musial before him and by Mike Schmidt years later. A muscled 200-pound, 5'9" frame and catlike reflexes made Campanella one of the most talented defensive catchers in baseball history; he handled rookie and veteran pitchers alike with a quiet confidence that was admired throughout the league.

In fact, Campanella did perhaps as much (in some ways more) for the acceptance of blacks in the big leagues, with his soft-spoken style and workhorse proficiency at the skilled catcher's position, as Robinson had done with his flamboyant baserunning and combative spirit. "Robinson was the trail blazer, the standard-bearer, the man who broke the color line . . ." wrote Red Smith, dean among American sportswriters. ". . . Campanella was the one who made friends." Campanella's true popularity with Brooklyn fans, teammates, and opposing players was attested by the outpouring of support that followed his accidental paralysis only months before the team's move westward. Baseball's single largest crowd ever — a throng of 93,103 gathered in Los Angeles Coliseum on May 7, 1959 — turned out for a benefit exhibition game between the New York Yankees and newly arrived Los Angeles Dodgers staged to honor the fallen hero from another city (Campanella had never played a game in Los Angeles) who may well have been the most popular ball player ever to proudly wear Dodger blue.

Harold "Pee Wee" Reese, the "Little Colonel" out of Ekron, Kentucky, will always be remembered as captain of the "Boys of Summer" teams of the early and mid-1950s. A brash Dodger rookie at the height of Larry MacPhail's

tenure in 1940, Reese was still around for one brief season in Los Angeles in 1958, a career spanning 16 big league campaigns and a full two decades of glory years in Brooklyn under MacPhail, Rickey, and O'Malley. Only twice did he lead the National League in individual offensive categories – 104 walks in 1947 and 132 runs scored in 1949 – yet the diminutive Reese was a perennial National League All-Star selection in the years between 1947 and 1954. The consummate team player, Reese always cheerfully sacrificed his abilities as a talented base stealer (he led the National League in 1952 with 30 and pilfered more bases than Robinson in six of the ten seasons they played together), since the Dodgers preferred hit-and-run style of play under managers Burt Shotton, Charlie Dressen, and Walt Alston.

It was as a flawless shortstop and quiet team leader, however, that Reese earned his Hall of Fame stature. After replacing fiery Leo Durocher at the keystone position in 1940, Reese remained the mainstay of the Dodgers' ever-evolving lineups under managers Durocher, Shotton, and Dressen. Throughout the 1940s he was Brooklyn's unsung hero and widely acknowledged MVP. Much has also been written about the quiet role of Reese as team captain and established clubhouse leader in paving the way for Jackie Robinson among his not always so accepting or racially tolerant teammates. But the incomparable hub of the Dodgers' greatest infields (those in which he was surrounded by Cox

and Robinson at third, Robinson and Gilliam at second, and Hodges at first) was above all else a consistent winner and an on-field leader by example, especially when the chips were down and a pennant or World Series was on the line. In his seven World Series appearances with Brooklyn, Reese hit a more-than-credible .272 (three points above his career average), he remains the all-time Dodgers leader in runs scored (1338), and still trails only Hall of Famer Zack Wheat on the Dodgers' career hit list (with 2170). Most remarkable of all, in a career noted for its longevity, is the fact that Reese often batted at both ends of the Dodgers order (lead-off or in the eighth slot) and yet only four men in Brooklyn franchise history (Snider, Hodges, Wheat, and Furillo) managed to knock in more runs.

One Brooklyn Hall of Fame hero remains – easily the noblest of them all. Edwin "Duke" Snider was the unfortunate victim of baseball's most baneful curse – the hopelessly unreachable standard of unlimited natural "potential." Over the course of 18 summers he socked 407 homers (5.7 roundtrippers every 100 at bats), clubbed 40 or more roundtrippers in five consecutive seasons (1953-1957), and amassed 2116 career hits and a lifetime .295 batting average. But for the Duke of Flatbush there were always unfilled expectations and easy justifications for so much more. He was moody throughout much of his career, renowned for sulking at his outfield post after a strikeout or missed hit-

Left: *Harold "Pee Wee" Reese earned his nickname from a remarkable boyhood proclivity for playing marbles, and not from his diminutive size. And there was certainly nothing at all diminutive about Pee Wee Reese's role once he donned Brooklyn flannels for the 1940 season. The acknowledged team leader for the better part of two decades, Pee Wee led the league once in runs scored and once in stolen bases, socked 126 homers from slots at both the top and the bottom of the batting order, and holds the ball club career standard with 1338 runs scored.*

Opposite top: *The noble "Duke of Flatbush" mugs for the camera alongside manager Chuck Dressen at the start of 1953 spring training camp. The four bats which Snider totes here are symbolic of the four circuit blasts he had provided during a previous fall's World Series loss to Stengel's Yankees. Dressen stands ready to offer a fifth symbolic bat in hopes of a repeat performance and a more positive outcome in the 1953 Fall Classic.*

Opposite bottom: *The end of an era is poignantly symbolized by a crippled Roy Campanella and an abandoned Ebbets Field, itself about to undergo a final assault of the wrecker's ball. The date here is February 23, 1960, and Campy is on hand with Carl Erskine and several additional teammates as the formal demolition of Brooklyn's longtime baseball palace is sadly but inevitably begun.*

ting opportunity; he often cursed the fans and avoided the media. His immense natural skills at the plate and afield were so great that he appeared to the casual fan never to be fully trying. Only Furillo, among the "Boys of Summer" Dodgers of the 1950s, possessed a more potent throwing arm, and Snider was once actually fined by management for injuring his arm while attempting to throw a ball clear out of the Los Angeles Coliseum during pre-game practice.

There were numerous injuries (especially a damaged knee) that slowed him, but these were never very visible nor fully acknowledged during his Brooklyn playing days, further contributing to the unfortunate image of a pampered and lackadaisical superstar. And then there was the presence of those other titans of the era — Mantle with the Yankees and Mays with the Giants — rival superstars also stationed in the glamorous center-field position and competing for equal attention in the cramped quarters of New York's baseball media glut. Yet Snider's skills were also incomparable. His longtime Dodger roommate Carl Erskine reports often shuddering with the thrill of watching the daily greatness of this future Hall of Famer. Snider's left-handed swing was flawless and he covered his outfield post with the silent speed of a gazelle. For those who saw him roam center field for a decade in Brooklyn, or witnessed him line countless towering drives over the Ebbets Field right field screen, there was never a more effortless or more graceful slugger nor a more nearly complete player in the game's history.

BROOKLYN DODGER ACHIEVEMENTS

ALL-TIME TEAM CAREER BATTING LEADERS

Games Played	Zack Wheat	2322
At Bats	Zack Wheat	8859
Hits	Zack Wheat	2804
Batting Average	Willie Keeler	.360 (1800 At-Bats)
Home Runs	Duke Snider	389
Runs Scored	Pee Wee Reese	1338
Runs Batted In	Duke Snider	1271
Extra Base Hits	Duke Snider	814
Stolen Bases	Mike Griffin	264
Doubles	Zack Wheat	464
Triples	Zack Wheat	171
Total Bases	Zack Wheat	4003

ALL-TIME TEAM CAREER PITCHING LEADERS

Innings Pitched	Brickyard Kennedy	2857
Wins	Dazzy Vance	190
Losses	Brickyard Kennedy	150
Earned Run Average	Jeff Pfeffer	2.31 (1100+ Innings)
Strikeouts	Dazzy Vance	1918
Bases on Balls	Brickyard Kennedy	1128
Game Appearances	Clem Labine	425
Games Started	Brickyard Kennedy	332
Shutouts	Nap Rucker	38

SINGLE-SEASON BATTING RECORDS

Batting Average	Babe Herman	.393 (1930)
Hits	Babe Herman	241 (1930)
Home Runs (Left)	Duke Snider	43 (1956)
Home Runs (Right)	Gil Hodges	42 (1954)
Runs Batted In	Roy Campanella	142 (1953)
Runs Scored	Babe Herman	143 (1930)
Most Sacrifice Hits	Jim Casey	32 (1907)
Singles	Willie Keeler	179 (1900)
Doubles	John Frederick	52 (1929)
Triples	Henry Myers	22 (1920)
Slugging Pct.	Babe Herman	.678 (1930)
Bases on Balls	Eddie Stanky	148* (1945)
Most Strikeouts	Dolf Camilli	115 (1941)
Fewest Strikeouts	Jim Johnston	15 (1923) (150 Games)
Extra Base Hits	Babe Herman	94 (1930)
Total Bases	Babe Herman	416 (1930)

*National League Record

SINGLE-SEASON PITCHING RECORDS

Wins	Joe McGinnity	29 (1900)
Losses	George Bell	27 (1910)
Earned Run Average	Rube Marquard	1.58 (1916)
Winning Percentage	Fred Fitzsimmons	.889 (1940) (16-2)
Strikeouts	Dazzy Vance	262 (1924)
Innings Pitched	Oscar Jones	277 (1904)
Game Appearances	Clem Labine	62 (1956)
Games Started	Oscar Jones	41 (1904)
Shutouts	Burleigh Grimes	7 (1918)
	Whitlow Wyatt	7 (1941)

DODGER HALL-OF-FAMERS

Brooklyn Dodgers in the Cooperstown Hall of Fame

Player	Position (Brooklyn Dodgers Years)	Inducted
Walter Alston	Manager (1954-57)	1983
Roy Campanella	Catcher (1948-57)	1969
Don Drysdale	Pitcher (1956-57)	1984
Burleigh Grimes	Pitcher (1918-26)	1964
Sandy Koufax	Pitcher (1955-57)	1972
Pee Wee Reese	Infielder (1940-42, 1946-57)	1984
Branch Rickey	General Manager (1943-50)	1967
Jackie Robinson	Infielder (1947-56)	1962
Wilbert Robinson	Manager (1914-31)	1945
Edwin (Duke) Snider	Outfielder (1947-57)	1980
Dazzy Vance	Pitcher (1922-32, 1935)	1955
Zack Wheat	Outfielder (1909-26)	1959

Additional Hall-of-Famers Who Played with the Brooklyn Dodgers

Player	Position (Brooklyn Dodgers Years)	Inducted
David Bancroft	Shortstop (1928-29)	1971
Dan Brouthers	First Base (1892-93)	1945
Max Carey	Outfielder (1926-29, 1932-33)	1961
Hazen (Kiki) Cuyler	Outfielder (1938)	1968
Billy Herman	Second Base (1941-43, 1946)	1975
Waite Hoyt	Pitcher (1932, 1937-38)	1969
Hughie Jennings	Infielder (1899-1900, 1903)	1945
Willie Keeler	Infielder (1893, 1899-1902)	1939
Joseph Kelley	Outfielder (1899-1901)	1971
George Kelly	First Base (1932)	1973
Henry (Heinie) Manush	Outfielder (1937-38)	1964
Walter (Rabbit) Maranville	Shortstop (1926)	1954
Richard (Rube) Marquard	Pitcher (1915-20)	1971
Thomas McCarthy	Outfielder (1896)	1946
Joseph McGinnity	Pitcher (1900)	1946
Joe (Ducky) Medwick	Outfielder (1940-43, 1946)	1968
Casey Stengel	Manager (1912-17, 1934-36)	1966
Arky Vaughan	Infielder (1942-43, 1947-48)	1985
Lloyd Waner	Outfielder (1944)	1967
Paul Waner	Outfielder (1941, 1943-44)	1952
John Ward	Manager (1891-92)	1964
Hack Wilson	Outfielder (1932-34)	1979

BROOKLYN DODGERS RETIRED UNIFORM NUMBERS*

*Numbers of Brooklyn ballplayers later retired by Los Angeles Dodgers

1	Pee Wee Reese	32	Sandy Koufax
4	Duke Snider	39	Roy Campanella
19	Jim Gilliam	42	Jackie Robinson
24	Walter Alston	53	Don Drysdale

BROOKLYN DODGER NO-HITTERS

Date	Pitcher	Opponent	Score
July 31, 1891	Thomas Lovett	New York	6-0
June 2, 1894	Edward Stein	Chicago	1-0 (6 innings, rain)
July 20, 1906	Malcolm Eason	at St. Louis	2-0
September 5, 1908	Nap Rucker	Boston	6-0
September 13, 1925	Dazzy Vance	Philadelphia	10-1
August 27, 1937	Fred Frankhouse	Cincinnati	5-0 (7 innings, rain)
April 30, 1940	James Carlton	at Cincinnati	3-0
April 23, 1946	Edward Head	Boston	5-0
September 9, 1948	Rex Barney	at New York	2-0
June 19, 1952	Carl Erskine	Chicago	5-0
May 12, 1956	Carl Erskine	New York	3-0
September 25, 1956	Sal Maglie	Philadelphia	5-0

POST-SEASON GAMES
LEAGUE TIE-BREAKING PLAYOFFS

Year	Opponent	Wins-Losses	Dodgers Manager
1946	St. Louis Cardinals	St. Louis 2, Brooklyn 0	Leo Durocher
1951	New York Giants	New York 2, Brooklyn 1	Charlie Dressen

Tied for First, Playoff for National League Championship

WORLD SERIES

Brooklyn Dodgers – 1 World Championship, 9 National League Championships

Year	Opponent	Wins-Losses	Dodgers Manager
1916	Boston Red Sox	Boston 4, Brooklyn 1	Wilbert Robinson
1920	Cleveland Indians	Cleveland 5, Brooklyn 2	Wilbert Robinson
1941	New York Yankees	New York 4, Brooklyn 1	Leo Durocher
1947	New York Yankees	New York 4, Brooklyn 3	Burt Shotton
1949	New York Yankees	New York 4, Brooklyn 1	Burt Shotton
1952	New York Yankees	New York 4, Brooklyn 3	Charlie Dressen
1953	New York Yankees	New York 4, Brooklyn 2	Charlie Dressen
1955	New York Yankees	Brooklyn 4, New York 3	Walter Alston
1956	New York Yankees	New York 4, Brooklyn 3	Walter Alston

Right: *The end of an era was now at hand during spring 1958 as controversy continued to swirl regarding the Dodgers apparent plans to relocate to a new West Coast home. While "B" still appeared on Dodger uniform caps at the Vero Beach training camp, the beloved Bums would never again head north when winter weather broke. Reese and Zimmer here take a brief moment's rest from their preseason practice sessions to second the sentiments of a trio of long time Dodger rooters.*

YEAR-BY-YEAR STANDINGS AND SEASON SUMMARIES

Brooklyn Dodgers (1890-1957); team also called by such names as Trolley Dodgers, Superbas, and Bridegrooms, throughout 1890s, and known as the Brooklyn Robins (after manager Wilbert Robinson) from 1914 to 1931.

Year	Pos.	Record	Pct.	Margin	Manager(s)	Pennant Winner
1890	1st	86-43	.667	+ 6	William McGunnigle	Brooklyn
1891	6th	61-76	.445	−25½	John Montgomery Ward	Boston
1892	3rd	95-59	.617	− 9	John Montgomery Ward	Boston
1893	6th*	65-63	.508	−20½	Dave Foutz	Boston
1894	5th	70-61	.534	−20½	Dave Foutz	Baltimore
1895	5th*	71-60	.542	−16½	Dave Foutz	Baltimore
1896	9th*	58-73	.443	−33	Dave Foutz	Baltimore
1897	6th*	61-71	.462	−32	William Barnie	Boston
1898	10th	54-91	.372	−46	William Barnie	Boston
–	–	–	–	–	Mike Griffin	
–	–	–	–	–	C.H. Ebbets	
1899	1st	101-47	.682	+ 8	Ned Hanlon	Brooklyn
1900	1st	82-54	.603	+ 4½	Ned Hanlon	Brooklyn
1901	3rd	79-57	.581	− 9½	Ned Hanlon	Pittsburgh
1902	2nd	75-63	.543	−27½	Ned Hanlon	Pittsburgh
1903	5th	70-66	.515	−19	Ned Hanlon	Pittsburgh
1904	6th	56-97	.366	−50	Ned Hanlon	New York
1905	8th	48-104	.316	−56½	Ned Hanlon	New York**
1906	5th	66-86	.434	−50	Patsy Donovan	Chicago
1907	5th	65-83	.439	−40	Patsy Donovan	Chicago**
1908	7th	53-101	.344	−46	Patsy Donovan	Chicago**
1909	6th	55-98	.359	−55½	Harry Lumley	Pittsburgh**
1910	6th	64-90	.416	−40	Bill Dahlen	Chicago
1911	7th	64-86	.427	−33½	Bill Dahlen	New York
1912	7th	58-95	.379	−46	Bill Dahlen	New York
1913	6th	65-84	.436	−34½	Bill Dahlen	New York
1914	5th	75-79	.487	−19½	Wilbert Robinson	Boston**
1915	3rd	80-72	.526	−10	Wilbert Robinson	Philadelphia
1916	1st	94-60	.610	+ 2½	Wilbert Robinson	Brooklyn
1917	7th	70-81	.464	−26½	Wilbert Robinson	New York
1918	5th	57-69	.452	−25½	Wilbert Robinson	Chicago
1919	5th	69-71	.493	−27	Wilbert Robinson	Cincinnati**
1920	1st	93-61	.604	+ 7	Wilbert Robinson	Brooklyn
1921	5th	77-75	.507	−16½	Wilbert Robinson	New York**
1922	6th	76-78	.494	−17	Wilbert Robinson	New York**
1923	6th	76-78	.494	−19½	Wilbert Robinson	New York
1924	2nd	92-62	.597	− 1½	Wilbert Robinson	New York

Left: *Howie Schultz, Pee Wee Reese, and Ed Stanky here pose as the starting Brooklyn infield alongside new first sacker Jackie Robinson, moments before Robinson's historic big league debut in Ebbets Field on April 11, 1947*

Opposite: *Three stalwarts of the memorable "Boys of Summer" – Roy Campanella (l), Carl Furillo (c) and Carl Erskine (r) – pose in colorful splendor on their 1953 Bowman bubble gum cards.*

Year	Pos.	Record	Pct.	Margin	Manager(s)	Pennant Winner
1925	6th*	68-85	.444	−27	Wilbert Robinson	Pittsburgh**
1926	6th	71-82	.464	−17½	Wilbert Robinson	St. Louis**
1927	6th	65-88	.425	−28½	Wilbert Robinson	Pittsburgh
1928	6th	77-76	.503	−17½	Wilbert Robinson	St. Louis
1929	6th	70-83	.458	−28½	Wilbert Robinson	Chicago
1930	4th	86-68	.558	− 6	Wilbert Robinson	St. Louis
1931	4th	79-73	.520	−21	Wilbert Robinson	St. Louis**
1932	3rd	81-73	.526	− 9	Max Carey	Chicago
1933	6th	65-88	.425	−26½	Max Carey	New York**
1934	6th	71-81	.467	−23½	Casey Stengel	St. Louis**
1935	5th	70-83	.458	−29½	Casey Stengel	Chicago
1936	7th	67-87	.435	−25	Casey Stengel	New York
1937	6th	62-91	.405	−33½	Burleigh Grimes	New York
1938	7th	69-80	.463	−18½	Burleigh Grimes	Chicago
1939	3rd	84-69	.549	−12½	Leo Durocher	Cincinnati
1940	2nd	88-65	.575	−12	Leo Durocher	Cincinnati**
1941	1st	100-54	.649	+ 2½	Leo Durocher	Brooklyn
1942	2nd	104-50	.675	− 2	Leo Durocher	St. Louis**
1943	3rd	81-72	.529	−23½	Leo Durocher	St. Louis
1944	7th	63-91	.409	−42	Leo Durocher	St. Louis**
1945	3rd	87-67	.565	−11	Leo Durocher	Chicago
1946	2nd‡	96-60	.615	− 2	Leo Durocher	St. Louis**
1947	1st	94-60	.610	+ 5	Burt Shotton	Brooklyn
—	—	—	—	—	Clyde Sukeforth	
1948	3rd	84-70	.545	− 7½	Leo Durocher	Boston
—	—	—	—	—	Burt Shotton	
1949	1st	97-57	.630	+ 1	Burt Shotton	Brooklyn
1950	2nd	89-65	.578	− 2	Burt Shotton	Philadelphia
1951	2nd‡	97-60	.618	− 1	Charlie Dressen	New York
1952	1st	96-57	.627	+ 4½	Charlie Dressen	Brooklyn
1953	1st	105-49	.682	+13	Charlie Dressen	Brooklyn
1954	2nd	92-62	.597	− 5	Walter Alston	New York**
1955	1st	98-55	.641	+13½	Walter Alston	Brooklyn**
1956	1st	93-61	.604	+ 1	Walter Alston	Brooklyn
1957	3rd	84-70	.545	−11	Walter Alston	Milwaukee**

* Tie
** World Champion
‡ Tied for 1st, but lost post-season playoff series
Finishes since 1900: First-10; Second-8; Third-8; Fifth-8; Sixth-14; Seventh-7; Eighth-1; First Division-28; Second Division-30.

INDEX

Numbers in *italics* indicate illustrations